julia bradbury's
WAINWRIGHT
WALKS

*I'd like to thank my family and friends (you know who
you are) for their ever-present support and encouragement.
Thank you of course to AW for leaving behind such
a legacy and to Clare Jones for your interpretation of the
stories and the landscape. I dedicate this book to my son
Zephyrus who has spun our lives around with his smiles,
to our lost friend Mark Weir from the Lake District who
is watching us from the big sky, and to Professor Jay
Appleton for his inspirational qualities as a human being
and knowledge of life. Thanks also to everyone at
Frances Lincoln for their publishing patience!*

Frances Lincoln Ltd
4 Torriano Mews
Torriano Avenue
London NW5 2RZ
www.franceslincoln.com

British Library Cataloguing in Publication Data
A catalogue record for this book is available from
the British Library.

ISBN: 978-0-7112-3379-9
Printed and bound in China

9 8 7 6 5 4 3 2 1

Pages 2-3: Blencathra's saddleback summit from the east
Right: Ullswater at dawn on a misty autumn morning

CONTENTS

Blencathra, Sharp Edge (detail)

'The fleeting hour of life of those who love the hills
is quickly spent, but the hills are eternal.'
Alfred Wainwright

Walking and having an opinion about our countryside are national pastimes in this country and we're pretty good at both. The wonderful and absurdly talented author Bill Bryson said at a recent gathering that if you were in mid-America on a Sunday afternoon and bellowed: 'Right we're all off for a walk across some farm land now', the entire room would think you were bonkers. But we Brits have a special connection with our landscape, and without sounding fanatical or crazed I think we should do what we can to protect, nurture and appreciate it.

It is quite curious that of all the television programmes I have worked on and made over the last fifteen years, it is Wainwright Walks that has generated the most communication and comment: A television series featuring me following in the footsteps of Alfred Wainwright, following Alfred Wainwright's own television series in the 1980s where he followed in his own footsteps. It isn't something that could have been planned or predicted but I am proud to be that woman standing in such deep manprints.

Julia at Helm Crag

Julia and the crew with Catbells' summit in the background

It all began with an unrelated meeting at the BBC with a commissioner called Richard Klein in which we coincidentally talked about walking. Do you enjoy walking (as in hiking)? Yes. Favourite place? The Peak District because my father Michael was born there, I went to school in Sheffield, and he fired up my passion for the outdoors by taking me out across the Peaks from the age of about 6. Do you know who Alfred Wainwright is? Of course. There were a few Wainwrights on the heavily laden bookshelves at home and my best mate is from the Lake District. I somehow managed to come across as reasonably coherent and not too desperate, because he went away from our meeting and saw *Watchdog* which I was presenting at the time, and noticed that I could actually walk and talk simultaneously, albeit across a studio. Bingo! So I went for another meeting with the executive producer Eric Harwood and we couldn't stop gassing. We still can't stop gassing to this day.

'There's man all over for you, blaming on his boots
the fault of his feet.'
Samuel Beckett

Contrary to opinion I don't spend my entire life roaming
around the countryside in sturdy boots and Gortex. I love
the outdoors, landscapes and the natural world, and the
conundrum of our expanding population versus the need
to protect our areas of greenness and biodiversity is a
constant source of intrigue, but I do happen to believe that
some people can spend *too* much time outdoors. I relish
the diversity of my job and enjoy the challenge of climbing
mountains one week, taking part in a science project the next
and investigating consumer affairs the week after. Having
said that, Wainwright definitely merged a hobby with my TV
career and set part of me off in a new direction, for which I
am very grateful. I'm proud to be a woman in these shoes.
Let's face it ladies, men are better at a whole range of other
sports; cricket, football, weight lifting, but not curling or more
importantly, walking.

WALK : *The ordinary human gait in which both feet
are never off the ground at once.*
WALKING : *The act of going on foot : act of moving
with a slow step.*

If I had one piece of advice for anyone embarking on hiking as their newfound hobby, it would be to get walking boots professionally fitted. Even if you're a hardened hiker – go for a re-fit. Running shoes should be changed every 8,000 miles; hiking boots are about the same. My feet are crumbling. I have trouble with my heel bone (calcaneus) so I use orthotics (specialist insoles) to correct my abnormality. They can help with flat feet, heel pain, shin pain and leg pain by slightly altering the angles at which the foot strikes the ground. But there is no point using them with old knackered boots! They're not for everyone however, so if you feel any pain take your boots to an Orthotist to ensure you get the appropriate insole. If the pain is more than just a niggle then go and see a specialist rehab Physio to check your biomechanics (walking pattern) and to give you some exercises.

I break my boots in on a treadmill or wear them for weeks around the house after work. DO NOT GO FOR A LONG WALK IN A BRAND NEW PAIR OF WALKING BOOTS. You're asking for trouble and the world's worst blisters.

'There is no love sincerer than the love of food.'
George Bernard Shaw

I have a healthy appetite and I need plenty of nutrition (and chocolate) when I'm out there on the hills, but I'm not big on sandwiches. The say beware Greeks bearing gifts (I'm partly Greek on my mother's side) but I am about to share a much-loved family recipe for Keftaides – Greek meatballs, which make a fantastic packed lunch. Delicious hot or cold they travel well and you can make a batch for consumption over a number of days. Take a little pot of home made tzatsiki up the mountain with you and you'll make more friends than Sarah Palin at a tea party (which Wainwright wouldn't have liked because he preferred walking alone).

For the Tzatsiki you'll need:

350g/12oz Greek yoghurt

1 cucumber

2 tbsp lemon juice

2 cloves of garlic, grated finely

dash of extra virgin olive oil

fresh dill to taste, chopped

Mix together the yoghurt, cucumber (I leave the skin on and slice into thin strips), lemon juice and garlic in a bowl. Add the olive oil and chopped fresh dill. Chill before you pack it and pack some pittas too. Yum.

Keftaides

500g minced beef (or vegetarian substitute)

1 small onion, chopped finely

2 small cloves of garlic, chopped finely

2 slices white bread

120ml red wine

1 egg, beaten

1 tbsp fresh mint, chopped finely

1 tbsp parsley, chopped finely

½ tbsp dried mint

salt & pepper

1tsp cinnamon

100g parmesan cheese, grated finely

flour

olive oil

Blend the bread in a food processer until you have small breadcrumbs. Then mix the onion, garlic, mint, parsley, cheese and cinnamon into the breadcrumbs. Add this mixture to the mince. Season and add the egg and red wine. Mix everything together.

Cover the bowl with a cloth and put in the fridge to chill. Form into meatballs approximately 4cm in diameter. Coat the meatballs in flour and fry in hot olive oil until browned (make sure the centre of the meatball is cooked). Transfer to a paper towel, and repeat with the remaining meatballs.

'I may not have gone where I intended to go, but I think I have ended up where I needed to be.'
Douglas Adams

I am not going to tell you what to pack in your backpack but I will implore you not to get lost. Therefore whatever guidebook, waterproofs and food you take with you, please jam an OS map and a compass in your stuff as well. I have worked and filmed with a lot of Mountain Rescue teams around the country. These volunteers are quite literally lifesavers who deal with over a thousand calls a year. The incidents range from unfortunate to life threatening. Around 14% of all Mountain Rescue call outs are 'lost or overdue' incidents. Tell people where you're going, when you think you're going to be back and assume your mobile won't work. The Lakes are particularly bad for phone signal. Which can be good. Total escape.

Julia with an RAF rescue team at Helvellyn

'Many are they who have fallen under the spell
of Lakeland, and so many are they who have been moved
to tell of their affection, in story and verse and picture
and song.'
Alfred Wainwright

Newspaper articles exist a'plenty, Wikipedia will give you
the run down, Hunter Davies has dedicated 356 pages to
him in his biography, and when our Wainwright Walks series
was commissioned by the BBC in 2006, AW was enjoying
something of a renaissance. The man himself would shudder
to think he was 'fashionable'.

Perhaps strangely for a bloke so obsessed with an area,

View from Orrest Head

he wasn't born in the Lake District and he didn't live there in his younger years either. He visited for the first time in 1930 at the age of twenty three – a relative late starter to rambling. He arrived with his cousin Eric on the bus from Blackburn about sixty miles away. Their first view was from the summit of Orrest Head 'It was a moment of magic, a revelation so unexpected that I stood transfixed, unable to believe my eyes.' The love affair had started. I don't know about you but I adore that moment of satisfaction when you make it to the top of a summit, that first glance out into the landscape and beyond, you are caught up in the spectacle of the moment, swimming in a pool of ocular delights.

AW's head was turned. This working class lad, born the youngest of four in Blackburn (in 1907) would never be the same again. It is curious how a single moment can change the course of your life forever. A bit like my meeting with Richard Klein at the BBC.

Wainwright wrote over fifty books in his lifetime but it is his seven *Pictorial Guides* to the Lake District where he beautifully and obsessively details 214 fells that bring us together. What is extraordinary about his achievements is that he created all his books while he held down his day job. In his own memoir *Ex-Fellwanderer* published in 1987, AW wrote: 'My father, a stonemason, was an alcoholic when he had any money...' Family life was troubled, so despite being a bright pupil he left school at thirteen to head out to work to help the family, starting out as an office boy at Blackburn Town Hall. He studied accountancy at night school and eventually became Borough Treasurer. Never trust someone entirely if they can understand double entry bookkeeping I say, but as we now know there was more to him than numbers and bureaucracy. Hunter Davies describes the seven guides as 'not merely guidebooks, but philosophical strolls...conceived and created as a total work of art.' In 1941 Wainwright secured a position as an accountancy assistant in Kendal's Borough Treasury department, a demotion at work but the achievement of a lifetime – to be located in The Lakes. It was eleven years later aged forty-five that AW worked out a plan to spend the next thirteen years writing about the Lakeland fells, which he now knew intimately from his solitary walks. Can you imagine planning that far ahead? I don't even know what we're having for dinner on Wednesday!

It mustn't be forgotten that Alfred married Ruth Holden in 1931. It's fair to say that theirs was not a happy marriage. They had a son called Peter (whom Wainwright became estranged from later in life) and they didn't talk much. He would head off to the Lakes to escape the marriage and there is a strong argument to suggest that had they been happier, he wouldn't have walked or written as much. If anything. They divorced in 1968 and two years later he married his love Betty McNally, with whom he had 'struck up a friendship' over many years. They did talk, and walk together.

In 1966 the seventh and final *Pictorial Guide* came out – bang on schedule. A week early in fact.

Just what you'd expect from this imaginative, curmudgeonly, obsessive personality.

'Just living is not enough... one must have sunshine, freedom, and a little flower.'
Hans Christian Anderson

Nobody can deny the beauty of the Lake District. 500 million years of geological processes have produced a physical landscape of mountains and lakes of immense scenic beauty. Folding, uplifting, glaciers and melt water have created a unique topography. The Lake District includes smooth U-shaped valleys and steep, sharp ridges, England's highest mountain and deepest and longest lakes. It's often compared to a wheel, with the core located just north of Grasmere at Dunmail Raise. The valleys and lakes radiate outwards as the 'spokes'.

Haweswater
from the third cairn

This grandeur and greatness has inspired poets and artists for centuries; the Lakeland Poets, William Wordsworth, Samuel Taylor Coleridge, and Robert Southey (who supposedly wrote *Goldilocks and the Three Bears* as a thank you to Coleridge for allowing him to stay with him) were all stimulated by the scenery. Beatrix Potter, the creator of one of the most famous rabbits of all time would write and draw inexhaustibly at her Hill Top Farm near Ambleside. Many have fallen prey to the charms of the lakes, not least of all 'Red' (Betty's nickname for Wainwright).

Wainwright died in 1991, for many, a legend in his own lifetime, and still to this day. His carefully observed pocket sized guidebooks covering his walks across virtually all of the Lakeland fells are still essential companions for walkers and lovers of The Lakes. Written in a no-nonsense northern way they are beautifully illustrated by AW himself, in a style reminiscent of nineteenth century etchings.

Although AW has been dead for over twenty years his popularity and name is, if anything, even greater today. Perhaps this is due to the explosion of interest in outdoor pursuits and rural tourism, combined with a large dollop of nostalgia – and a yearning for a more tranquil lifestyle. AW himself was also a television personality as I've mentioned, particularly known for his *Coast to Coast* broadcast in the company of Eric Robson, a long-term friend of AW and still a countryside fan and exponent to this day.

However, when I was fortunate enough to present the 'new' Wainwright Walks in 2006/7, I quickly came to realise and respect the groundswell of affection and interest still latent with the Great British outdoor-loving population. This series and the *Coast to Coast* series which followed, have proved incredibly popular and enduring – with many repeats – and a still growing fan base of all ages! Actually membership of the Wainwright Society has gone up from 100 in early

Julia with her trusty Pictorial Guide *(Book Two) on High Street*

2003 to the current figure of 1,400 since the programmes were broadcast for the first time and the number of hits on the AWS website has increased from 200,000 per month in 2007 to 462,000 per month in the year after the broadcasts. I was proud to be made an honorary member in 2008 at the Society's AGM in Staveley before a walk to the summit of Reston Scar on a bright and sunny Saturday morning.

Although I did not meet AW himself, I do feel the Wainwright Walk series have provided a connection to the man and his times. My one direct link was my short meeting with AW's widow Betty, towards the end of her life when she gave her seal of approval to my interpretation of AW's works. I was also privileged to provide a reading at AW and Betty's memorial service in 2009.

The saying 'life goes on' certainly applies to the legend and legacy of AW. I hope reading this book brings back old memories or provides some new ones. As a prelude to each walk I have included some thoughts and reminiscences as well as some background events which occurred during the making of each programme. Dip into these walks wherever your fancy takes you but you could start with a trip to the last resting place of AW's ashes on Haystacks. Watch where you're putting your feet.

Travel within the Lake District

Although most people use a car as transport in the Lake District it is possible to access all the walks by public transport, Wainwright did after al! Bus timetables are seasonal so please use the following websites to plan your journey around the Lakes:

http://www.cumbria.gov.uk/roads-transport/public-transport-road-safety/transport/publictransport/busserv/default.asp

http://www.golakes.co.uk/information/getting-around-cumbria.aspx

http://www.keswick.org/visitor-information/getting-to-keswick/transport-in-keswick/

Drew Whitworth's blog http://214wainrights.word-press.com/ is definitely worth a read as he takes on his project of completing all 214 Wainright Walks without using a car.

HAYSTACKS

Julia's Overview

Haystacks was Wainwright's favourite fell and he remains forever part of it since his ashes were scattered near Innominate Tarn. It was therefore, quite fitting that Haystacks should be our first 'telly walk'. For weeks I'd been doing my AW research, reading all about him, trying to get the fullest picture of him in my mind. He's quite a unique man and there isn't anyone else I can think of in this country who is so synonymous with one place. Wainwright is the Lake District and the Lake District is Wainwright.

When you ask people about him, 'curmudgeonly' is a word that pops up a lot, but there is so much more. Eric Robson spent time with Wainwright, walking, talking and filming the original television series in the 1980s. Eric is a Lake District local, writer and broadcaster, so who better to meet for a spot of advice before embarking on my own Wainwright wanderings. When that moment came, there he was, standing in the drizzle with a shaggy dog and a tall well-worn walking stick.

A couple of things particularly stood out to me from that conversation. Eric described Haystacks as being a mountain that had a 'spirit'. It's just one word but it really does seem to capture so much about this very special place with all its craggy outposts, dramatic views and secluded interludes of water. Now that AW's ashes are scattered 'somewhere up there' his spirit and the spirit of the mountain seem bound as one.

Eric also talked about the popularity of Wainwright's guides and how they are still as much in demand as ever

Julia Bradbury takes in the peaceful surroundings at Innominate Tarn
Pages 22-23: Innominate Tarn, Haystacks. AW's final resting place

before. You could certainly argue that they are not the most modern, or flashy handbooks and yet millions of people still use his words and pictures to guide themselves across the fells. Perhaps this is because nobody has interpreted mountain landscapes better. Wainwright wasn't simply a good artist, he was a man who clearly loved the Lakes and these books are his tribute to that landscape. As Eric said 'these are *not* guidebooks – they are works of philosophy and poetry.'

That was quite a lot to take up the mountain for the first time with a new crew, for a new series. Ah well, barely anyone would be watching ... (or so we all thought at the time).

HAYSTACKS

ASCENT FROM GATESGARTH
2,000 feet of ascent : 3 miles

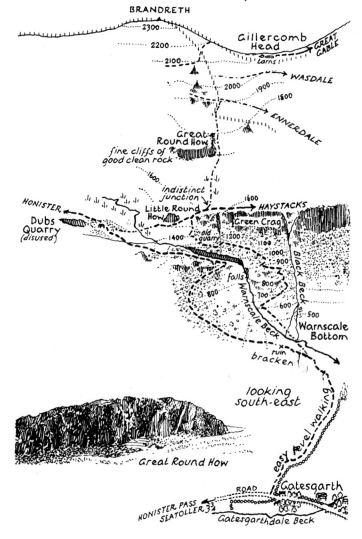

BRANDRETH

2300

2200

Gillercomb
Head

GREAT
GABLE

2100

tarns

2000   1900

WASDALE

1800

ENNERDALE

Great
Round How

fine cliffs of
good clean rock

1600

indistinct
junction

1600

HONISTER

Little Round
How

HAYSTACKS

Dubs
Quarry
(disused)

Green Crag

1400

old
quarry

1200

Black Beck

1100

1000

900

falls

800

800

700

800

600

500

Warnscale
Bottom

ruin
bracken

looking
south-east

easy level walking

Great Round How

ROAD

Gatesgarth

HONISTER PASS
SEATOLLER 3½

Gatesgarthdale Beck

THE WALK
Haystacks – from Gatesgarth

SUMMIT HEIGHT: 1,958 feet/597 metres
(1,550 feet/472 metres of ascent)
DISTANCE: 1¼ miles/2.81 kilometres
OS MAP: OL4
Pictorial Guide Book Seven – The Western Fells

'...the ascent of Haystacks via the pass of Scarth
Gap is a prelude of much merit and beauty to a
mountain walk of much character.'
A. Wainwright

OVERVIEW

This walk starts at a point known as Gatesgarth Farm, nestled on the edge of Buttermere. The path takes you across farmland at the southern end of the lake and then the initial ascent is a short but steepish climb northwest before the path turns sharply and heads southward through bracken-covered slopes. The path then cuts along the edge of the hillside, giving spectacular views into the valley below, before reaching the flatter parts known as Low and High Wax Knott. You then head across a zigzag path at Scarth Gap, where the terrain becomes rocky underfoot, before reaching a grassy saddle from where you can gain a clear view of the summit ascent. You approach the peak via a small un-named tarn where you will find a summit cairn and some breathtaking views.

The Walk

'Haystacks stands, unabashed and
unashamed in the middle of a circle of
much loftier fells, like a shaggy terrier
in the company of foxhounds.'
A. Wainwright

Haystacks from Buttermere

Haystacks rises between the deep hollow of Warnscale Bottom and Ennerdale. Once you've left the valley floor at Gatesgarth this is a walk which seems to start with a bang. For my first Wainwright outing, I have to admit, I was expecting a more gradual climb from the beginning. But only just a few minutes into the walk proper you make some quick height to about 500 feet (152 metres), gaining some pretty instant and engrossing views. This climb certainly did the trick in awakening my senses and also my muscles and I got to experience that rather hot and slightly sweaty feeling you get from the first climb of the day. Down below, Buttermere with its silken waters really did look refreshing.

So, for my first Lakeland excursion things got off to a good start. The weather looked like it was going to hold, there was a chink of beautiful blue sky and I hadn't got lost. But as I was to learn in the course of my television adventures in Wainwright's footsteps, Lakeland is known for its changeable weather patterns, each valley almost having its own microclimate. Even the most experienced of walkers can be caught unawares by a sudden burst of rain or low mist creeping in.

Not only was this my first Wainwright fell, a test in itself to see whether I would even make it to the top, but these were also my first tentative steps in learning about the man who was so entirely motivated by these surroundings. Wainwright describes his passion for this landscape in the first of his *Pictorial Guides*: 'The magical atmosphere of the Lakes. The silence of lonely hills. The dawn chorus of birdsong. Silver cascades, dancing and leaping down bracken steeps. And the symphonies of murmuring streams.' These were all attractions that I was beginning to see unravel before me on my walk.

The view of Buttermere from where this walk begins at Gatesgarth Farm

It wasn't too long after the first steep section that I had to have a rest to catch my breath, have a sip of water and start to take in these new surroundings. Across the valley rays of light were breaking through the cloud, playing a merry dance across the heathland and for me it was magic. I was starting to see why Wainwright, who was office-bound all week, loved to escape to this. The peace, quiet and scenery were beautiful.

Wainwright always argued that you should walk alone. He didn't like the distraction of other people. He especially didn't like gangs of schoolchildren. I might have said that was a bit unsociable, but actually on this first walk being able to taste just a bit of that peace and tranquillity and having all that space to myself felt like a real luxury.

The next major landmarks are Low and High Wax Knott where Wainwright warns: 'It is a test of iron discipline to pass without halting several large comfortable boulders athwart the path.' If you take a peek across the valley from here you might also be able to pick out another path in Warnscale Bottom, which can also take you to the top of Haystacks.

Sheep at Gatesgarth Farm, Buttermere (passed on the walk up to Haystacks)

In the book there are actually six different ways to get to the top, so no chance of getting bored.

In Book Seven of his *Pictorial Guides* Wainwright speaks very favourably of the route from Gatesgarth via Warnscale Bottom: 'For sustained interest, impressive crag scenery, beautiful views, and a most delightful arrangement of tarns and rocky peaks, this short mountain excursion ranks with the very best.' Although this route takes you on a longer ascent of 2¾ miles, Wainwright liked the imposing crag overhanging the path. He would then enjoy the views on this walk as he made his leisurely descent.

Impressive views looking down onto Buttermere and Crummock Water

Next, you will approach Scarth Gap where the terrain becomes much rougher underfoot and the path also widens. Actually you can't really see the path. What was once an 'S' shape up the mountain has, in the words of Wainwright, been 'butchered' by short-cutters. But it is still a rewarding spot to get to as AW notes: 'Scarth Gap is one of the pleasantest of the foot-passes. Apart from the steep section above the sheep fold, the gradients are gentle and the views both above and behind are full of interest.'

Wainwright marks the top of Scarth Gap with a triangle indicating that you should find a significant cairn. On this, my first outing into the fells, cairns were a whole new discovery. So, for anyone else who may be new to fellside wandering, cairns like this are familiar sites in the mountains, made by the simple act of adding a stone as you pass and used as navigational aides to keep you on track.

Julia enjoys some of the sumptuous views to be gained from the summit

Hopefully you won't be making use of it for that purpose and from the grassy saddle you should gain a clear view of all the surrounding fells. It's lovely and soft underfoot here. Further to the south is Kirk Fell, but more importantly, up ahead will hopefully be a clear view of the climb to the summit.

In his first guide, Wainwright acknowledged the attraction of this landscape: 'Many are they who have fallen under the spell of Lakeland, and so many are they who have been moved to tell of their affection, in story, verse, picture, and song.' As I started to close in on my first summit these words began to ring a little more true. I too was starting to fall under the magic of the Lakes.

Big Stack,
looking east from
a point near the path
to the summit from
Scarth Gap.

An aerial view back down the valley to the start of the walk.

At this point of the walk, look out for cracking views back down onto Buttermere and Crummock Water. On a clear day you may even be able to see all the way to the Solway Firth in Scotland. Wainwright always maintained that he began writing the guidebooks for his own memory of the places he had visited and loved, something to look back on when he could no longer walk the fells. From the opening sentence of Book One, his motivation was clear: 'Surely there is no other place in this whole wonderful world quite like Lakeland. No other so exquisitely lovely. No other so charming. No other that calls so insistently across a gulf of distance. All who truly love Lakeland are exiles when away from it.'

It was on Haystacks that AW took his final walk with eyesight that had deteriorated too far for it to be safe for him to wander alone any longer. He famously said: 'Haystacks wept tears for me that day.' It's amazing to think that Wainwright was still walking when he was nearly eighty. In those final steps towards the summit I was certainly starting to appreciate why AW was so enchanted with Haystacks.

As he so rightly said: 'Here are sharp peaks in profusion, tarns with islands and tarns without islands, crags, screes, rocks for climbing and rocks not for climbing, heather tracts, marshes, serpentine trails, tarns with streams and tarns with no streams. All these with a background of magnificent landscapes, await every visitor to Haystacks but they will be appreciated most by those who go there to linger and explore.' For my first jaunt into the fells this walk had certainly opened my eyes to all those wonderful natural charms.

AW also said that for a man trying to get persistent worry out of his mind, the top of Haystacks is a wonderful cure. Stepping onto your first summit does sort of momentarily suspend things. Everyday life can be put aside whilst an expansive view rolls out below. It provoked a surprising set of feelings for me, conjuring both exhilaration and excitement at the achievement, but also that wonderful sense of stillness, of just being there, in the elements, enjoying that one special moment.

Note the profile in shadow. Some women have faces like that.

perched boulder on a rock platform

This summit is more than a peak and a cairn. There are three tarns, plunging edges of rocky crags and sumptuous views from every vantage point. Wainwright describes this as, 'in fact, the best fell-top of all, a place of great charm and fairyland attractiveness.'

The summit tarn

You may wish to make time for a small summit detour to visit AW's truly final destination – Innominate Tarn. Such was his love of Haystacks, it was the place where he chose to have his ashes scattered following his death in 1991, aged 84. He'd made his affection for this spot very clear: 'All I ask for at the end is a last long resting place by the side of Innominate Tarn, on Haystacks, where the water gently laps on the gravelly shore, and the heather blooms, and Pillar and Gable keep unfailing watch. A quiet place; a lonely place.

I shall go to it for the last time and be carried. Someone who knew me in life will take me there, and empty me out of a little box, and leave me there alone.

And if you, dear reader, should get a bit of grit in your boots as you're crossing Haystacks in years to come, please treat it with respect – it might be me.'

For me this walk was a fantastic introduction to Wainwright and his world of fell wandering. Of all 214 fells in the Lake District, Haystacks clearly captured his heart *and* his imagination and it's very easy to see why. Wainwright said: 'A walk in Lakeland is like a walk in Heaven.' This was the end of my first Wainwright but only the start of my explorations and already I was starting to see just what he meant.

The view down on Haystacks from Honister

Julia's tips for a tipple:

With its slate floors Wasdale Head Inn (Wasdale) is definitely a fellwanderer-friendly establishment. I can recommend the food, choice of traditional ales and great atmosphere which celebrates where British mountain climbing began.

Other options include Yew Tree Coffee House (Seatoller) and The Fish Inn (Buttermere).

BLENCATHRA

Julia's Overview

Blencathra is a beauty and after Haystacks it felt like a real mountain. At 2,847 feet (868 metres), it is firmly in the big league of English fells. The plan for the series was to meet people 'along the way' and punctuate the walks. My first on-camera chat that day was with Chris Jesty.

Whilst it's already been acknowledged that the *Pictorial Guides* do not come under the contemporary section, they have been recently re-issued as revised editions. Chris Jesty has completed ALL 214 fells following in the footsteps and eyes of AW, correcting and revising details that have changed along the way, so, a perfect interviewee to fill in the gaps. These kind of chats normally take about an hour to film. For reasons I can't quite explain nearly three hours later we were still standing next to the A66. Chris has so much knowledge and enthusiasm on the subject and those elusive sound bites that you need to make sense of it all remained just that, elusive. Eventually we had what we needed and finally I asked about Blencathra's Big Moment (most fells have them) – Sharp Edge. What's it like? Were you frightened? Do you have any tips for tackling the ridge? 'Ooo no, I didn't do Sharp Edge – I went round it' was the reply. Not the most reassuring response!

There is no doubt that Wainwright truly loved this fell. He spent months dedicating himself to any given mountain, finding every single way to the top, discovering every route, exploring each ridge and hidden corner. He would even sleep on it to make sure he could cover as much ground as possible during those research trips. But I wanted to know why AW loved Blencathra so much and why out of all 214

The familiar view of Blencathra that many visitors see from the busy A66, which skirts along at its feet
Pages 38-39: Blencathra and Threlkeld village

fells he devoted a staggering thirty-six pages to it, more space than he gave to any other. And I had two days (minus three hours) to do it. That's all the time (i.e. budget) we had for each fell: two days, one cameraman (Jan Ostrowski), one sound lady (Clare Edmans), one director (Owen Rodd), one runner, one guide (David Powell-Thompson) and sometimes one executive producer (Eric Harwood).

Tackling this fell, 'a mountaineer's mountain', via the rather notorious Sharp Edge route was a 'must', despite its rather intimidating name. After all, this was one of those places Wainwright so firmly applauded in the final pages of Book Seven. Not only does AW include Blencathra as one of his favourite fells, but he also lists Sharp Edge amongst his six favourite places to be, apart from summits. So, tackling the ridge, with all its rather vertigo inducing possibilities, just had to be done. And I didn't want to get crag-locked. This was the next step up for me, (and quite a big one, at that). For once it was a beautiful day...

BLENCATHRA

ASCENT FROM SCALES
via SHARP EDGE
2250 feet of ascent : 2¾ miles

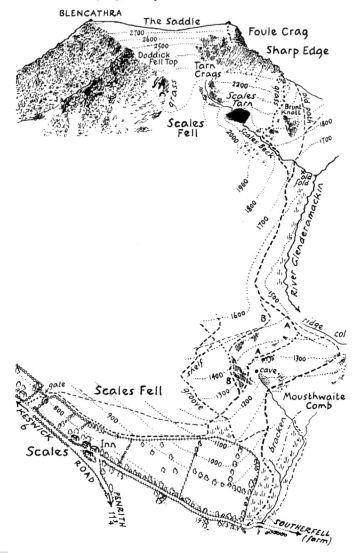

BLENCATHRA

The Saddle

2700

2600

2500

Doddick
Fell Top

Foule Crag

Sharp Edge

Tarn
Crags

2200

Scales
Tarn

Brunt
Knott

1800

Scales
Fell

grass

grass

1700 Pike

1700

Scales Beck

2000

1900

1800

1700

old
fold

River Glenderamackin

1600

B

A

ridge

col

shelf

groove

A

cave

B

1400

1300

1300

1200

gate

Scales Fell

Mousthwaite
Comb

800

900

bracken

KESWICK

Inn

1100

Scales

ROAD

1000

PENRITH
11¼

SOUTHERFELL
(farm)

42

THE WALK
Blencathra – from Scales via Sharp Edge

SUMMIT HEIGHT: 2,847 feet/868 metres
(2,250 feet/686 metres of ascent)
DISTANCE: 3¾ miles/6 kilometres
OS MAP: OL5
Pictorial Guide Book Five – The Northern Fells

'...most of all it is a mountaineer's mountain.'
A. Wainwright

OVERVIEW
Starting from the Inn at Scales Village you leave the main road behind. To begin, there's a steady ascent through the dense bracken of the lower fell. Things then get steeper as you reach the side of the great hollow known as Mousthwaite Combe. The path zigzags up the side of the Combe before edging its way round the top of the rim. At the top of the Combe, the route heads north at a crossroads, following the valley of the Glenderamackin River. From here, you should be able to get a clear view of the mountain's summit and the distinctive plateau top that lends the mountain its alternative name – Saddleback. Leaving the river, there's a short ascent to the secluded Scales Tarn. The tarn is a perfect resting spot and also the access point for Sharp Edge. The Edge is the shortest, most direct and perhaps the most treacherous approach to any peak in The Lakes. But once along it your reward should be a gentle and very satisfying stroll across the saddle to the peak.

The Walk

'This is a mountain that compels attention, even from those dull people whose eyes are not habitually lifted to the hills.'
A. Wainwright

An aerial view of Blencathra

One of the first things you notice about Blencathra is what a great big hulk of mountain it actually is. It's definitely got a slightly intimidating look about it with all its different slopes, ridges, and dark crevices. The next obvious thing you notice is probably the big fat A Road right at the foot of the mountain, the A66, which I suspect Wainwright would have hated.

When he published his Blencathra guide in 1962, this road was nothing but a plan in the minds of local authorities. But Wainwright made his opposition perfectly clear: 'The present road policy in the Lake District, of generally turning highways into racetracks, is surely wrong. It is an offence against good taste to sacrifice their character to satisfy speeding motorists and roadside picnickers.'

But Blencathra remained a very important fell for Wainwright. People who knew him claim that this was the only fell Wainwright truly completed. In the winter of 1960 he devoted himself to climbing and mapping it, research which contributed to the staggeringly comprehensive thirty-six-page description.

Back at the A66, the reward of its summit can seem a long way away. It's a pretty decent climb but you'll probably be looking forward to getting started and heading away from the noise of the road. However, perhaps because of this rumbling highway, Blencathra is now one of the most familiar landmarks in Lakeland. Today, motorists speed along past its base taking in its splendid position. It stands alone, the last great outpost in the region and for those who venture up its flanks it provides views right across to the Pennines.

To begin with at least, it really is a gentle climb as the path meanders round the edge of Mousthwaite Combe. The next

An aerial view of the start of the route from Scales

landmark to look out for is a sort of mini crossroads. A faint path can be spotted coming up the hill and a stronger one across the mountain. But at this point you've got to follow the Glenderamackin River.

The whole atmosphere of the walk changes round about here. You tip over into the heart of the valley and suddenly the road noise has gone and all you can hear is the river gushing through the valley down below and the odd sheep. It's lovely. I suspect the day I had on Blencathra is exactly the sort of day in the fells Wainwright would have loved. There I was striding out through a beautiful valley, blue skies above and not a soul in sight.

Despite nineteen million visitors a year, The Lakes still offer one of England's best opportunities for escapism. And that was half the appeal for Wainwright. He wrote: 'I do prefer my own company to that of other people...the tinkling of a mountain stream, the twittering of birds, the sound of wind sighing across the mountain tops – that's music to me.'

It's not too long before you get a view of Sharp Edge, looking exactly like it does in Wainwright's drawing, its

An aerial view of the secluded Scales Tarn

unmistakable jagged silhouette looming dramatically upwards. From here it almost looks impossible to climb, but you may well be able to see walkers up ahead, making their way across, like little 'ants' on the top. From here on Blencathra begins to feel like a truly considerable mountain.

For the walker in search of a raw fell-climbing experience, Blencathra scores highly. The Lakes these days are littered with specially constructed footpaths, a necessary step to protect the fells from tens of thousands of visitors every year. Blencathra, for now at least, remains amazingly free from manmade paths, leaving you to enjoy the mountain, just as Wainwright first found it.

from Scales Tarn

Arriving at Scales Tarn at the base of Sharp Edge delivers a classic bit of Lake District landscape. There seems something so magical about being next to such tranquil water and it's the perfect spot for lunch. Scales Tarn is

An aerial view of the dramatic Sharp Edge, Blencathra's jagged ridge of rock.

one of hundreds of tarns in this area. They're a real feature of the Lake District and mark the spot where huge basins of snow and ice once gathered. Many of these became so large that they spilled over to form glaciers that carved out so much of Lakeland. Over ten thousand years later, the ice has long gone and all that remains are these great natural bowls, where water gathers, forming a tarn. Sitting next to Scales Tarn can make you feel like a speck of dirt by a plughole in an enormous basin. It's a really imposing spot, a bit like a giant amphitheatre.

One thing you will also notice from down here is that as craggy as Sharp Edge looks, once you've made it across it's completely flat along the top which leads to the final summit spot. But reading Wainwright's guide will leave you in no doubt about the challenge that lies ahead: 'Sharp Edge is a rising crest of naked rock, of sensational and spectacular appearance, a breaking wave carved in stone. The sight of it at close quarters is sufficient to make a beholder about to tackle it forget all other worries, even a raging toothache.

The crest itself is sharp enough for shaving (the former name was Razor Edge) and can be traversed only at some

Blencathra, Sharp Edge

risk of damage to tender parts.... There is one awkward place calling for a shuffle off a sloping slab onto a knife-edge. Countless posteriors have imparted a high polish to this spot.'

When I tackled Blencathra for my television series it was still pretty early days in my Wainwright wanderings and I was still definitely finding my feet. The prospect of something as substantial as Sharp Edge was therefore understandably a little intimidating. So rather than attempt to tackle this section single-handedly I had the great fortune to be able to enlist the support and guiding service of my very own 'mountain goat' – David Powell-Thompson.

David is one of those sure-footed men of the hills who has been roaming these parts for the best part of his life. When asked how well he knew the fells he simply answered in his inimitably understated way 'Oh, pretty well'. Once I found out

An aerial view of the Edge with Scales Tarn in the background

he'd celebrated his last birthday by running 48 miles across thirty peaks I knew I must be in safe hands. An incredible feat, made even more surprising because it was undertaken to celebrate his sixtieth birthday.

For me, it was just a really steadying experience to have company, as we slowly started to wend our way upward. Wainwright always liked to send people ahead first so they saw things for the first time. So, in keeping with this David sent me up front, reminding me to keep three points of contact and to enjoy myself (sometimes a little harder when the wind picked up, adding an extra frisson of excitement).

The ridge, for me, felt like a decent challenge and one that required some concerted effort and concentration. You too may find that the main section passes relatively quickly as you dig down and slowly wend a route along its craggy folds. The next landmark to aim for is Foule Crag, the final steep climb to the summit plateau but another challenge in itself. It's a slightly more exposed spot, where, if you are anything like me, you'll find you want to use hands and feet to steady yourself. Again, it may require a bit of a 'deep breath' for those of us who aren't so fond of heights but, if you take it slowly and stay concentrated on each little footstep, you soon advance across. If you can bear to look up and around it's worth taking a moment to soak up some of the tremendous views you get here. From this point you can certainly see that Sharp Edge is deserving of its name as a string of jagged rocks cut the horizon below.

Foule Crag
Sharp Edge
Brunt Knott

Unlike David, I'm no real rock-climber, so there was definitely a sense of achievement in completing something that felt truly adventurous. Having got over Sharp Edge, I felt that I really began to know what Wainwright meant when he called Blencathra 'a mountaineer's mountain'.

Getting to know this mountain a little more intimately also helped seal the question of its name. Once you've scaled Foule Crag you have one final stretch to go across the saddle, which has given this fell its alternative name. Saddleback was the Victorian title given on account of its distinctive shape, but Blencathra is the ancient name. For me, there's just something more dramatic about this older name. It seems to roll off the tongue with a certain smoothness. Wainwright would only have Blencathra, noting however that the fell was 'unfortunately' better known as Saddleback.

Once you arrive on top, the reward for your vertiginous efforts is a really magnificent panorama. You can pick out

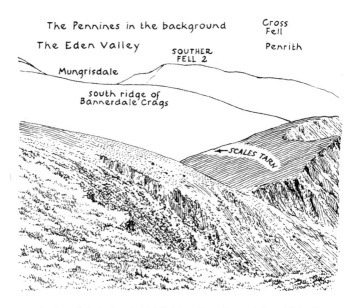

The Pennines in the background   Cross Fell

The Eden Valley   SOUTHER FELL 2   Penrith

Mungrisdale

south ridge of Bannerdale Crags

←SCALES TARN

plenty of Lakeland highlights, like the mighty Helvellyn, Skiddaw, and Skiddaw Little Man and then just above Derwentwater there is Catbells, a real favourite with lots and lots of people who go to Keswick. The view then runs up onto Dalehead, Hind Scarth and Robinson; the list just goes on.

Whether you know the peaks or not, the view from nearly 3,000 feet (914 metres) up is undeniably spectacular and you feel utterly detached from the world below.

This may not be the highest spot in the Lakes, but it's one of the best known and as I discovered, it's certainly one of the toughest climbs around.

Wainwright wasn't very impressed with the cairn, which marks the actual top. He states: '...nothing marks the highest point but a poor untidy heap of rubble. On occasion attempts are made to give the thing some shape and dignity, but until someone carries up a few decent size blocks, the cairn will continue to disappoint by its insignificance.'

We know however, that Wainwright thought this fell worthy of more pages than any other, but we'll never truly know whether Blencathra might just have been his *all time* favourite. AW was canny enough to keep this sort of information a close secret. But with this fell he really did leave behind a very comprehensive guide to one of the Lakes' most dramatic climbs and left us in no doubt that whilst there are many saddlebacks there is only one Blencathra.

Julia's tips for a tipple:

The White Horse Inn (Scales) is walker-friendly with good food and traditional ales.

There is also The Mill Inn (Mungrisdale) where the crew and I enjoyed an excellent roast lamb dinner and Jan the Cameraman demonstrated his marrowbone-sucking skills to the crew.

Julia's Overview

Just when I thought I was getting a handle on Wainwright and his walks then along came a complete surprise. Castle Crag was everything I'd so far come to think a Wainwright walk wasn't. It was mostly low-level, it didn't need a full day to tackle it and it didn't feel all that wild and far flung. In fact, it seemed wonderfully accessible. Joyfully, no dawn chorus start – I am truly terrible in the mornings and my communication consists of some grunts. I can't even do breakfast too early, so wherever we camp I request a bacon sandwich on brown, with ketchup, wrapped in foil please and I normally only take my first bite at around 10am. The combination of a later start and some good tunes in the car on the way to our start point in the village of Grange meant that the entire team were on good form that day.

Having only just really discovered the fells, I did wonder if I was going to feel a little bit short-changed with this walk. I'd gained a bit of summit fever and had already started to long for those wilder windswept tops that felt so far removed from the hustle and bustle of life down below in the valleys. Castle Crag is bit of a blip on the landscape rather than a mighty mountain. At only 951 feet (290 metres) it hardly registers in scale against some of its loftier neighbours. But here's the nub of it. Castle Crag might be small but that doesn't mean it can't be spectacular. Wainwright once again came up trumps picking this spot. This walk really helped me appreciate just how much AW had reached into Lakeland's hidden corners. So here was another lesson learned from the

An aerial view of Castle Crag, Borrowdale and Derwentwater
Pages 54-55: Castle Crag from above Grange

great man; great fells come in all shapes and sizes. Jan our cameraman had a saying when there was a particularly fine view ahead of him: 'Ooooh that's an expensive shot – cost you extra.' Since doing these walks I've been lucky enough to see the summit of Castle Crag from a helicopter a few times, and it's definitely expensive.

CASTLE CRAG

ASCENT FROM GRANGE

700 feet of ascent
1½ miles

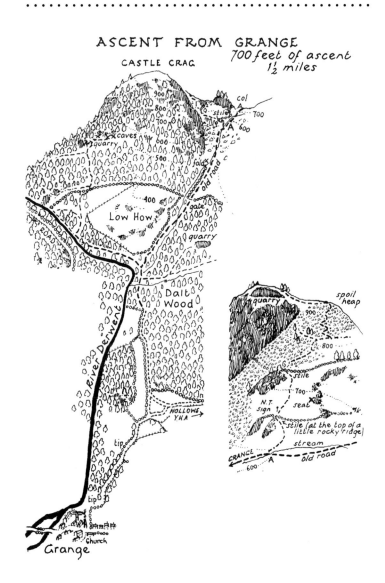

THE WALK
Castle Crag – from Grange

SUMMIT HEIGHT: 951 feet, 290 metres
(700 feet/213 metres of ascent)
DISTANCE: 1½ miles/2.4 kilometres
OS MAP: OL4
Pictorial Guide Book Six – The North Western Fells

'Whether time permits or not on no account miss the little riverside walk below Low How. Here are the most beautiful reaches of the Derwent.'
A. Wainwright

OVERVIEW

Castle Crag is situated in the north western area of the Lakeland fells. It lies on the edge of Derwentwater and unlike my other walks this is largely a low-level valley walk. The walk begins at the picturesque village of Grange and progresses through Borrowdale. The first stage of the route is covered by woodland and follows the edge of the river. You then make your way across the National Trust campsite at Hollows Farm, before the woodland opens out at the mouth of the river. The path then turns off and heads southwards towards the old quarry road where the route is swamped by imposing crags on either side. The path then splits off and you follow a short sharp ascent up the cragside, navigating a zigzag path carved out of the slate spoil heap. This leads to the final ascent to a grass covered plateau and the professionally made summit cairn.

The Walk

'If a visitor to Lakeland has only two or three hours to spare, poor fellow, yet desperately wants to reach a summit and take back an enduring memory of the beauty and atmosphere of the district... let him climb Castle Crag.'
A. Wainwright

Castle Crag from above Grange

As the third walk in my Wainwright explorations this offered something entirely different. It really is a gentler walk (well to begin with at least). You spend the first half-mile meandering along a country lane, but take care to keep an eye out for what lies up ahead. You should be able to spy a view of Castle Crag with its craggy outcrops and shroud of trees, which looks like a sort of lost world waiting to be discovered. The crag itself is a mini-mountain, with a lush tree-covered top, it's quite magical actually, which certainly makes it perfect as a family walk.

When Wainwright wrote Book Six, the Ordnance Survey hadn't determined the altitude of the summit at Castle Crag. By comparing the horizontal planes of surrounding fells to the east and west, Wainwright quoted the height as 985 feet (300 metres). But the official height today is actually recorded as 951 feet (290 metres). We might think a few feet of difference doesn't matter too much but this is exactly the kind of detail that Wainwright was obsessed with (and probably would have hated to find he'd not got exactly right).

The path runs alongside the River Derwent, which winds its way through the Borrowdale Valley. Wainwright calls Castle Crag an obstruction in the throat of Borrowdale, as it forces the river through a narrow gap, before widening so it can continue on to feed into Derwentwater. After about ten minutes you are away from the road and heading through the woods, where you will start to feel the gentle ascent of this walk begin.

There is definitely something fairytale-like about this place. Maybe it's the cloaking wood and the silence and stillness it seems to bring. But that's the great thing I've started to realise, no two walks in the Lakes are the same. Even the same fell can be experienced in so many different ways. When Wainwright walked he would make notes, but

The view of Castle Crag from Borrowdale

he never drew in situ. Instead he would painstakingly create sketches from the photographs he took on his walks, fitting them together to get the whole view of a mountain range, or the entire summit view. Using just pen and ink he was able to bring his Lakeland walks to life as detailed illustrations.

Although a solitary and fiercely private man, Wainwright was known for his dry sense of humour, which on occasion he would drop into his writing. Book Six begins with this interesting dedication: 'To those unlovely twins, my right leg and my left leg staunch supporters that have carried me about for over half a century, endured much without complaint and never once let me down.

Nevertheless they are unsuitable subjects for illustration.'

Getting back to the walk, you will want to keep an eye out for this next section. You emerge from the densely packed wood and pop out through a gate and into an altogether different scene of craggy, grey, open rock faces. It's really quite a different walking experience. Instead of having great views all around you as with the higher-level walks, these imposing crags tower over you instead.

An aerial view of Borrowdale, the low-level start point of the walk.

This is really where you get a sense of history of this part of the lakes. Formerly a walling stone quarry, Castle Crag is now a silent reminder of a once thriving industry.

Wainwright described the spot as being 'pitted with cuttings and caverns and levels, every hole having its tell-tale spoil heaps'.

As a civil servant, Wainwright was in the enviable position of being able to enjoy the fells for pleasure. For the local quarrymen the fells and lakes were part of an altogether more industrial landscape. It was a place where they would work long and gruelling hours for the equivalent of around twelve and a half pence a day in today's money.

In addition, the Lake District is also known for its temperamental weather. The Borrowdale Valley is in fact the wettest valley in England, with an average rainfall of 140 inches per year. Mist, cloud and horizontal rain, all familiar to the Lake District, can make any walk hazardous (even a low-level one like this. As I had started to learn on my walks, there was a golden rule to rambling and that was, 'never leave home without your waterproofs').

Once you get to around 400 feet (122 metres) the walk gets a little bit steeper, but the bonus is that the views are amazing and you should be able to spy Derwentwater. Although this landscape might seem rather barren with all its shards of grey slate there is a certain dramatic beauty to it without a doubt. As Wainwright's description suggests, the passage of time has helped to soften this scene: 'Its abrupt pyramid, richly wooded from base almost to summit but bare at the top is a wild tangle of rough steep ground, a place of crags and scree and tumbled boulders, of quarry holes and spoil dumps of confusion and disorder. But such is the artistry of nature, such is the mellowing influence of the passing years that the scars of disarray and decay have been transformed in a romantic harmony, cloaked by a canopy of trees and carpet of leaves.'

During my walk my sights were firmly set on Castle Crag but a detour from the Quarry Road would lead to a series of caverns. The most famous of all being known as Millican Dalton's Cave. At the end of the nineteenth century Dalton

Millican's Cave

abandoned his job as an insurance clerk in London for a life of adventure and freedom. The call of the wild led him to take up summer residence in a massive cave on Castle Crag. He was a self-titled 'Professor of Adventure' as well as a vegetarian, pacifist and teetotaller. He became known as the 'Borrowdale Hermit' and the words carved on his cave read: 'Don't waste words, jump to conclusions'.

Interestingly Wainwright himself acknowledges that Castle Crag is not strictly a fell in its own right. He describes it as a 'protuberance on the rough breast of Scawdel'. What it might lack in height it makes up for in other ways. It certainly offers an ideal introduction to walking in Wainwright's Lakeland by starting gently and gradually building upwards (and whilst there may not be the altitude of a big ascent there's some sharp hard work at the end that will definitely get the legs going). Wainwright helpfully offers these words of wisdom for the novice walker in Book Six: 'The first lesson that every fellwalker learns and learns afresh every time he goes on to the hills, is that summits are almost invariably more distant, a good deal higher and require greater effort than expected. Fellwalking and wishful thinking have nothing in common.'

As you gain more height what rears up ahead looks like a strange rocky maze. This precarious spoil heap represents exactly one of the aspects of the fells that Wainwright was fascinated by – the traces of man on the landscape. This quarry was operating until the 60s with the quarrymen using gunpowder to blast the slate and this impressive spoil heap would have developed over decades as the fell was excavated.

An aerial view of Castle Crag's rocky profile showing the zigzag path to the summit

Continuing to head upwards to around 600 feet (183 metres) and the climb certainly feels worthy of a bigger fell (you'll definitely get the blood pumping). You should be able to look down onto the village of Rosthwaite, which was where the quarrymen would have lived. Snaking through the middle of the village is the road Wainwright would have travelled on. He famously didn't drive, and travelled all around the Lake District on buses.

Wainwright's passion for this lovely valley was abundantly clear in his chapter on Castle Crag: 'It encloses one mile of country containing no high mountain, no lake, no famous crag, no tarn, but in the author's humble submission, it encloses the loveliest square mile in Lakeland, the Jaws of Borrowdale.'

The next, rather odd landmark, is the quarry area itself where groups of slate appear to have been constructed in separate little piles. I have to admit it was ever so slightly

The summit·quarry

The pedestrian path to the
top goes up the grass
on the right

summit

Quarries and caves of Castle Crag

eerie, almost like some sort of odd graveyard. In fact, no one is really sure if the stones were laid out like this for a reason, or even when they appeared. They are regularly cleared away but nevertheless mysteriously continue to reappear. If you take a peek around here, you can also see where the quarrymen carved into the summit taking some impressively large chunks of the fellside out.

From here you can make your way to the actual top. The highest point on this summit is a mound of rock, which has been crowned by a professionally-made round flat-topped cairn. Below it, set in the rock, is a war memorial to the men of Borrowdale.

Wainwright suggests this was where an ancient British fort once stood, but warns: 'It needs a trained eye to trace any earthworks – which, in any case, must have been severely disturbed by an old quarry that has cut a big slice out of the summit and be it noted constitutes an unprotected danger.

An aerial view of the professionally made summit cairn

Photographers (who have a habit of taking backward steps when composing their pictures) should take care lest they suddenly vanish.' There may not be an awful lot of space once you get up there, but there is plenty to take in, including a spectacular view of Derwentwater backed by Skiddaw.

This is definitely a walk that introduces you to all that is best about Lakeland and can be perfectly slotted into a morning or afternoon. Castle Crag may be less than 1,000 feet (305 metres) and covered by the scars of man's impact, but it's a perfect little gem and I think it's truly deserving of its special status as the smallest fell to make it into Wainwright's *Pictorial Guides*. As Wainwright so wonderfully stated: 'Castle Crag is so magnificently independent, so ruggedly individual, so aggressively unashamed of its lack of inches...' In this case, less is certainly more.

THE SUMMIT

Julia's tips for a tipple:

This route isn't overly blessed with choices for your post-climb pint but the Scafell Hotel (Rosthwaite) will do you a pint although you might have to take your boots off at the door. There are also two tearooms in Grange and plenty of choice back in Keswick if you can wait that long.

SCAFELL PIKE

Julia's Overview

In preparation for the series I did the unthinkable. I bought new boots. My old ones definitely wouldn't have survived the entire run. But as every outdoor spod will tell you – new boots are the devil's friend. They need to be broken in. They must be 'at one' with your feet or it's blisters and chafing all the way. So I got them weeks before we started filming, determined not to come undone. As it happened I was in the Middle East where there aren't many mountains to climb so the treadmill at the gym had to do the job. There I was, surrounded by lycra-clad bodies, pounding the machine in my yoga outfit and heavy duty walking boots. I had one thing in my mind as I racked up the miles: Scafell Pike.

There was a new sense of trepidation. This was, after all, the biggest fell I had ever tackled in my explorations so far. It was only my fourth Wainwright outing and there I was, catapulting towards a new and far more demanding mountain experience.

There is a thrill to all of this, which I was starting to get a taste for. It's partly wrapped up in the unfolding nature of the day, each footstep taking you closer you hope, to the end – a genuine will we/won't we cliffhanger.

A lot of work goes into the programmes before we set foot on a fell. Research to work out the most interesting nuggets of history or geography and a recce to find the best places to stop and deliver at pertinent PTC (piece-to-camera). And of course the views are important too. I do my homework before each outing and try and get a sense of the story and the mood of each walk – as well as trying to memorise significant locations and people. Sometimes things pop into your mind and you just talk. At other times it's

Julia Bradbury soaks in the views from the Scafell Pike summit
Pages 70-71: The Scafell range and River Esk across Great Moss

agreed that 'we'll stop here and say this'. As we made our way up Grains Gill (at about 2,000 feet) I was to point out the ravine up ahead and mention the sheer face of Great End. Except again and again I kept calling it Great Head without realising it. The crew were in stitches and when I finally got it right and gestured around me, our executive producer was standing behind me, messing up the shot. I think it took about six takes to get that PTC.

Before we set off up Scafell Pike I had the opportunity to meet one of this area's other great characters who was able to help set me on my way with a bit of inspiration. Jos Naylor is one of Lakeland's most famous fell runners. A local sheep farmer by trade, this is the man who ran up seventy peaks on his seventieth birthday and conquered all 214 Wainwright fells in just seven days.

Meeting him was one of those truly inspiring moments that you can always look back on. His feats in the fells go way beyond what I might ever hope to achieve. Typically understated he described his mission to run all of Wainwright's fells in one go as 'just being a nice thing to do,

just to remember him.' It's even more impressive when you realise Jos developed a throat infection during the last two days of his run and didn't eat anything. Meeting him was a great reminder that the fells can stir an exuberance in us all, a desire to go just that little bit further, explore just a bit more – which we certainly did.

Filming took much longer than anticipated and we didn't reach the summit until dusk, which meant we had to head

The Scafells from Bowfell Tarn

back down in the dark. I don't recommend it. Despite the lack
of light, on our way down we met some people attempting
the Three Peaks Challenge... going up. Madness!

SCAFELL PIKE

....

ASCENT FROM BORROWDALE *continued*
via ESK HAUSE
3,200 feet of ascent : 5½ miles from Seatoller

GREAT END

ESK PIKE
2700
2600
2500

Esk Hause

B

C D

2500
2400
2400
wall-shelter grass A
2300

D: Central Gully
C: South-east Gully

STY HEAD and WASDALE

GREAT LANGDALE

The summit here is ALLEN CRAGS

Ruddy Gill
2000
1900

2100

former path not much used now

1700

1400
1300
1200

fold

Grains Gill

old sheepfold

Black Waugh

STY HEAD

signpost

Stockley Bridge

Styhead Gill

River Derwent

gates

Seathwaite

400

The Borrowdale Yews
(Wordsworth's 'fraternal four')

Seathwaite Bridge

River Derwent

ROAD

Seatoller

ROSTHWAITE
1¼

bus shelter

HONISTER PASS

THE WALK
Scafell Pike – from Borrowdale via Esk Hause

SUMMIT HEIGHT: 3,210 feet/978 metres
(2,900 feet/884 metres of ascent)
DISTANCE: 5½ miles/8.8 kilometres
OS MAP: OL 4&6
Pictorial Guide Book Four – The Southern Fells

'The ascent from Borrowdale is pre-eminent, because not only is the scenery excellent throughout but there is the advantage of two interesting and well-contrasted routes, so that one may be used in ascent and the alternative in descent, the whole round, in settled weather, being perhaps the finest mountain walk in the district.'
A. Wainwright

OVERVIEW

The walk begins at the southern end of the Borrowdale Valley at Seathwaite Farm and then follows the River Derwent southwards up to Stockley Bridge. Things get steadily steeper as the valley narrows and the route heads up Grains Gill to a height of 2,000 feet (607 metres). At the top you can take a brief detour to Sprinkling Tarn set dramatically beneath the sheer face of Great End. Heading back on the route, there's a long and steady climb up to the plateau at Esk Hause, which can make for a lunch spot with views to remember. Turning westwards, you then pass round the back of Great End and finally get on to the rocky Scafell Ridge. This dramatic stretch takes you past the lower peaks of Ill Crag and Broad Crag before the last testing climb to the Pike itself.

The Walk

'... here is a mountain without doubt, and a mountain that is, moreover, every inch a mountain. Roughness and ruggedness are the necessary attributes and the Pike has these in greater measure than other high ground in the country – which is just as it should be, for there is no higher ground than this.'
A. Wainwright

Scafell Pike's rocky summit cairn, the peak Wainwright described as 'the one objective above all others'

At 3,210 feet (978 metres) Scafell Pike tops the charts of English peaks and offers perhaps the toughest of all Wainwright's challenges. I didn't feel I could fully appreciate Wainwright's Lakeland until I'd tackled its greatest fell. AW described the Pike as the one objective above all others... a mecca. But I also wanted to know why Wainwright thought this particular fellwalk was the finest of all.

Wainwright's recommended route starts at Seathwaite Farm near Seatoller village, right in the heart of the Lake District, (which is about a seven-hour round trip for most walkers). What you could find disconcerting about the start of this walk, is that you can't see the destination. It's such a mountainous area the summit goal is hidden behind a shield of other peaks.

From Seathwaite Farm the peak might only be three miles as the crow flies, but with so many twists, turns and other peaks to negotiate, you end up walking much further than that before you finally close in on the summit. Wainwright sums up the challenge in Book Four: 'The ascent of Scafell Pike is the toughest proposition the 'collector' of summits is called upon to attempt, and it is the one above all others that, as a patriot, he cannot omit.'

Stockley Bridge is the first major landmark to aim for on the route. Originally it was an important packhorse crossing between Borrowdale and the Wasdale Valley in the west. In the mid 60s the bridge was almost destroyed by storms but now it's fully restored and probably carrying more traffic than ever before. It's also your cue that things are about to get steeper.

An aerial view of Stockley Bridge

As you make your way up Grain's Gill don't be lulled into any false hopes. The high point that greets you at the top of the ravine is not a summit view. It is in fact Great End, which you will be skirting around (and certainly not the highest point of this walk). By now you've covered almost half the walk in terms of distance but as for height, it's a different story, there's still over 1,500 feet (457 metres) left to go.

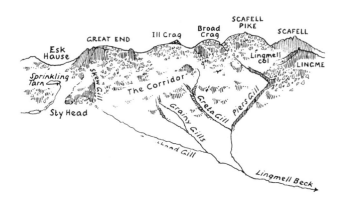

Sprinkling Tarn set dramatically beneath Great End

It's certainly worth taking in the views looking back down Borrowdale, on a good day you can just make out Castle Crag and Derwentwater behind. At the top of Grain's Gill Wainwright also recommends a detour. Sprinkling Tarn is one of this walk's little hidden gems. Lying just a few hundred yards off the main route and over a slight mound, it's visited by just a few of the thousands that trek up to Scafell Pike.

The silence here is magical, with maybe just the odd sheep, a little trickle of water or the flap of a raven's wing above disturbing the peace. Once you're here, the temptation is to linger as Wainwright pointed out: 'Too many walkers bound for Scafell Pike have given up the ghost here, daunted by the sight of Great End and bewitched by the beauty and solitude of the tarn.... 'Onwards!' must be the cry. Much remains to be done.'

Back on the route you'll reach the second ravine of the day, Ruddy Gill. So named according to Wainwright, because

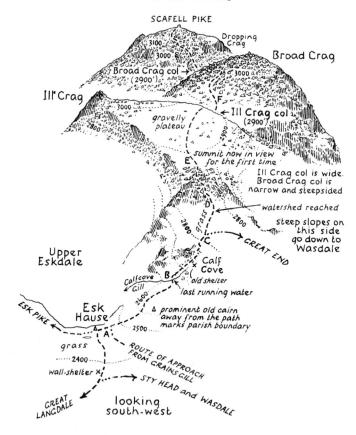

ASCENT FROM BORROWDALE
via ESK HAUSE

SCAFELL PIKE

3100
3000
Dropping Crag
Broad Crag col → (2900')
3000
Broad Crag
Ill Crag
3000
2800
gravelly plateau
F
← Ill Crag col (2900')
2900
summit now in view for the first time
E
Ill Crag col is wide. Broad Crag col is narrow and steepsided

D
watershed reached
2800
grass
2800
steep slopes on this side go down to Wasdale
GREAT END
C

Upper Eskdale

Calf Cove
B
Calfcove Gill
2600
old shelter
last running water

ESK PIKE ←
Esk Hause
A
prominent old cairn away from the path marks parish boundary
2500

grass
2400
ROUTE OF APPROACH FROM GRAINS GILL
wall-shelter ×
STY HEAD and WASDALE

GREAT LANGDALE
looking south-west

of the red subsoil. Whether you can see a red tinge or not the good news is it's a landmark of sorts, as you are now nearly at Esk Hause (which means you're at the top of the first page of the walk, see page 76).

You will now start to notice that the walk changes in character. The long view down the massive valley to Seathwaite Farm is gone, the gentle pastures are out of sight and you are up amongst the wild high fells. The path now leads straight to Esk Hause which at 2,500 feet (762 metres) is the highest pass in the Lake District.

Esk Hause has been an important pass for centuries and was used to transport wool from farms in Borrowdale to the Cistercian monastery at Furness Abbey, away to the south. It's amazing how the terrain suddenly becomes much more open here. With views down into three valleys it's a commanding, if utterly exposed spot.

From here you could once again be misled into thinking you can spy the summit. Many 'wishful thinkers' as Wainwright describes them, have mistaken Ill Crag for the peak. But no, there's still a mile and a half of the most difficult Lakeland terrain to negotiate. I love the way Wainwright describes Ill Crag as 'a desolate scene... a frozen avalanche of crags and stones, much of it unexplored or uncharted... a safe refuge for escaped convicts or an ideal depository for murdered corpses.'

Ill Crag, from the path above Esk Hause

After leaving Esk Hause the route crosses the grass to Calf Cove, where you climb up and onto the ridge that takes you right to the summit. (Just a word of warning though, this is where the legs start to burn). The Scafell Ridge is the most consistently high ground in England. For over a mile the path that runs from Great End, past Ill Crag, Broad Crag and ending in the Pike, never drops below 2,800 feet (853 metres). This desolate, volcanic rock is inhospitable yet also strangely captivating.

Up on the ridge it is just a giant boulder graveyard with sharp jagged rocks everywhere which makes for pretty challenging walking. Amongst this landscape the path completely disappears at times. The only clues to the route are the small cairns that other walkers have left behind. But Wainwright talks about the magic of camping out alone in a hollow just below here. He loved to watch the sunrise cast its pink glow over the dark crags and boulders. He wrote: 'Once in a while every keen fellwalker should have a pre-arranged night out amongst the mountains. Time drags and the hours of darkness can be bitterly cold, but to be on the tops at dawn is a wonderful experience and much more than recompense for the temporary discomfort.'

But for those who remain intent on reaching the summit in the same day there is one final hurdle to get over. As you edge along the ridge you will have the summit in your sights, only to find that you reach the end of the line and have to go down a sort of boulder highway to the bottom of a gap, and then all the way back up the other side to regain your height. It's just one of those things that the mountains seem to sometimes throw at you (especially when you are on your last legs).

It's when faced with this peak at close quarters that Wainwright poses an interesting question in his chapter on Scafell Pike: 'Why does a man climb mountains? Why has he forced his tired and sweating body up here when he might, instead, have been sitting at ease in a deckchair at the seaside? It is a question every man must answer for himself.'

*view
on the walk
from
Esk Hause
to the
summit*

But the climb back up is all that stands between you and the small matter of the top of Scafell Pike. (I suppose it's only fair that you have to work this hard to get to a peak this high).

Walking and filming certainly aren't conducive to any sort of speed walking so I'd been on the go for almost ten hours when I reached the summit. Wainwright rated this fellwalk as the very best and in one long day I'd seen everything the Lake District has to offer from wide valleys to steep ravines, silent tarns to windswept rocky ridges and conquered Wainwright's biggest climb. Wainwright, as you might expect sums it up rather nicely: 'Of the many routes of approach to Scafell Pike, this, from Borrowdale via Esk Hause, is the finest. The transition from the quiet beauty of the valley pastures and woods to the rugged wildness of the mountain top is complete, but comes gradually as height is gained and after passing through varied scenery both nearby and distant, that sustains interest throughout the long march.'

Reaching the summit of England's tallest mountain is certainly one of those moments where sheer exuberance breaks through. It's a good old slog to get here and everything feels like a worthy reward. From this lofty vantage point you

THE SUMMIT

can see hundreds of fells all around you and apparently on a really clear day, you can even see Blackpool Tower. For me though just being able to see this sea of summits unfolding before me was simply spectacular.

Wainwright says that fellwalkers are not attracted to this summit for its beauty, because it's not beautiful. It is sturdy and rugged and strong. It is simply the fact that this is the tallest mountain in England and when you get to the top... you can say 'I did it'.

There are places that my walks had so far taken me to where you'd be happy to spend hours and you'd choose to come again and again. But this spot has a very different quality. It's about being able to sit and look out across miles of cliffs and peaks, knowing you're above them all. There's really nothing quite like the feeling that you've conquered everything that was put in front of you.

Sunset views from the summit

Julia's tips for a tipple:

Wasdale Head Inn (Wasdale); The Old Dungeon Ghyll and The New Dungeon Ghyll, both in Langdale are all walker friendly, which is just as well in such a walking mecca.

HELVELLYN

Julia's Overview

Alfred Wainwright and I have something in common. We both walk in tweed? We're both partial to a pipe? We both have splendid sideburns? No… AW made his Helvellyn debut in adverse conditions back in 1930 and so did I more than seven decades later.

Helvellyn's 'Big Moment' is Striding Edge – the most famous spit on any mountain in Lakeland; 300 yards of exposed narrow ridge and a satisfying mountaineering achievement for most people. Ideally you can *see* it when you make your approach. The day started well, the weather was fine and we made good progress. I had a funny on-camera moment with a water bottle that wouldn't open (an out-take for the gag reel) and we pressed on. Then in the shake of a Herdwick's tail the dark clouds pulled up and the rain started to pour. We were too committed to turn around and David Powell-Thompson our guide and safety-man gave us the OK to continue. I donned a red waterproof jacket that didn't quite fit and David literally led me by the hand up and over the ridge. There are 'appalling precipices' on either side, which luckily I couldn't see otherwise I think I may have turned back.

Striding out from Patterdale earlier that morning accompanied by the twitterings of happy birdsong and the soft swish of swaying trees seemed an age ago. The initial optimism of the adventure had turned into bemusement and, to be honest, fear. I'd like to tell you about the people we met, the lunch we ate, some amusing moments but I can't remember a thing. I was so absorbed with the task at hand –

Julia battles the elements on Helvellyn
Pages 88-89: Helvellyn, looking to the summit from Striding Edge

not falling off – everything else has cleared from my mind.

On this walk I learned a lesson in the vagaries of Lakeland's weather. My walk went from blue skies to cloud and cloaking pea soup in nano-moments. Suddenly the soft rolling fells began to feel far more intimidating and menacing. But this is the lot of the fellwalker and a lesson in being prepared. On reflection (and after drying out) the experience was a reminder of the sheer richness of Lakeland walking, that really no summit is ever completely bagged or ticked off. To know a fell really does mean seeing it in all shades and colours, seasons and weathers. I can certainly now claim to have summited Helvellyn but truly knowing it is another matter. I have yet to see the summit in anything but rain.

HELVELLYN

ASCENT FROM PATTERDALE
2700 feet of ascent : 5 miles

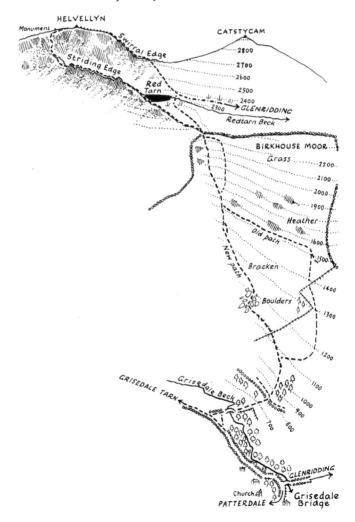

THE WALK
Helvellyn – from Patterdale via Striding Edge

SUMMIT HEIGHT: 3,118 feet/950 metres
(2,700 feet/822 metres of ascent)
DISTANCE: 5 miles/8 kilometres
OS MAP: OL5
Pictorial Guide Book One – The Eastern Fells

'Striding edge is the finest ridge there is in
Lakeland, for walkers - its traverse is always an
exhilarating adventure in fair weather or foul.'
A. Wainwright

OVERVIEW

My route starts from the church in Patterdale village, adjacent
to the Mountain Rescue Headquarters. The walk then heads
away from Ullswater taking a gentle walk along the floor of
the Grisedale Valley. As the leafy trees run out, the route
enters more familiar Lakeland terrain. For a mile and a half
a long path takes you to the well-known landmark known
as the Hole-in-the-Wall. This is where the drama begins. On
the right up ahead is the vast combe of Helvellyn, filled with
Red Tarn and encased by the mountain and its two ridges.
The start of Striding Edge is clearly marked by the rock
pinnacle of High Spying How. From here the famous Edge
rises and falls over numerous jagged peaks. As it meets the
bulk of Helvellyn, you are left with a steep scramble to the
plateau. The summit is then just a short walk away and the
drama of the climb turns into one of the flattest and gentlest
of Lakeland viewpoints.

The Walk

'Legend and poetry, a lovely name and
a lofty altitude combine to encompass
Helvellyn in an aura of romance.'
A. Wainwright

An aerial view across Ullswater

For me, this walk was about tackling two things; the mighty summit of Helvellyn and also Striding Edge, which Wainwright credited as the 'finest ridge in Lakeland'. At 3,118 feet, (950 metres) Helvellyn is the third highest peak in England. It enjoys a central location, numerous possible ascents, and the classic Striding Edge. 'There is no doubt that Helvellyn is climbed more often than any other mountain in Lakeland, and more than any other, it is the objective and ambition of the tourist who does not normally climb,' wrote Wainwright. AW came here as a twenty-three year-old in 1930. A complete newcomer to the Lakes, he arrived in Ullswater, determined to tackle Helvellyn the following morning.

Ullswater snakes southwards and ends in a dense mass of fells where you can just make out the flat summit of Helvellyn (and if I'm honest looking up it at from Patterdale it seemed a long, long way to the top).

St Patrick's is the parish church of what used to be known as Patrick's Dale and a rather tranquil start point for one of the area's toughest climbs. As you look up the valley of Grisedale, the village of Patterdale feels really protected on either side by the fells. But sadly, the two peaks you might initially spy are not the summit, they are just the approach slopes to Helvellyn.

Helvellyn is part of the most extensive range of high ground in England. For five miles a great succession of peaks line up, from Dollywagon Pike in the south to Great Dodd in the north. The ridge rarely drops below 2,500 feet (762 metres), with the summit of Helvellyn, the grand pinnacle, in the middle.

But before you need to tackle any serious climbing,

Grisedale & Ullswater (the usual route up to Helvellyn)

there's a good mile or so of single-track road to follow along the valley floor, before veering off onto a footpath which will take you up all the way up to the Hole-in-the-Wall. The route now firmly plants you in an area called Grisedale and it's just classic Lakeland scenery. Most of the land here has been part of a private estate for generations, which has preserved a selection of fine valley views that walkers will enjoy. The footpath is pretty much a straight diagonal plod up the southern flanks of the fell known as Birkhouse Moor.

As you climb, the views both in front and behind get better. Back over the top of Patterdale you look towards Lakeland's eastern-most summits, with the likes of High Raise and High Street ascending in the distance, fells

that Wainwright would go on to study in Book Two of his *Pictorial Guides*.

When you study a Wainwright Guide, there are certain things that you sort of come to expect, like the comprehensive drawings and very well laid out notes. But there were a couple of things in this description which I hadn't seen before, like the bullet-point notes about the various approaches. AW lists the options with some quick summaries like 'via Grisedale Tarn – a long easy walk on a good path', 'via Nethermost Pike – not for novices' and then (our chosen route) 'via Striding Edge – the best way of all'.

Something else I hadn't seen before were the graphs, which sort of plot the distance in relation to the altitude,

An aerial view showing Red Tarn and Striding Edge (left) and Swirral Edge (right)
Right: AW made his Helvellyn debut in adverse conditions and Julia's first ascent is no different

providing a measure of the steepness of the routes (very Wainwright to enjoy such obsessive detail). These don't feature in the other books so it's almost like he was trying things out in Book One.

The majority of walkers who attack Helvellyn's eastern side cannot fail to pass the giant wall that stretches from the valley floor in Grisedale up and along the entire ridge of Birkhouse Moor. Wainwright and his cousin encountered it for the first time, in less than perfect circumstances: 'We followed a pony route rising along the flanks of Birkhouse Moor above the lovely valley of Grisedale. The weather was less promising, and before reaching the gap in the wall we were enveloped in a clammy mist, and the rain started.'

The Hole-in-the-Wall as this spot is called, is quite a landmark and it really feels like a cut-off point; it's almost as

if one walk ends here and then another begins. The terrain changes completely. It's at this point that I would have had my first view of the summit, except on this occasion it was hidden under a layer of cloud. In typical Lakeland fashion the glorious weather of the morning had suddenly changed ushering in altogether more damp and misty conditions. But at least I could claim to be experiencing it as Wainwright first did (although I'm not sure if I wouldn't just have preferred the view).

From the Hole-in-the-Wall you progress until you are looking into the mouth of a great bowl with Red Tarn sitting right at the bottom and Striding Edge jutting upwards to your left.

Wainwright thought it a pity that the majority of walkers attacked the mountain from the opposite side. The smooth grassy slopes that rise out of Thirlmere are, he said, 'unattractive' and 'lacking in interest'. This side is geologically far more interesting, arguably a more difficult ascent, but as AW noted, this is the price you pay if you are to discover Helvellyn's 'true character'.

An aerial view showing the imposing Striding Edge with Ullswater in the background

Standing beneath Striding Edge is a sort of mini-geography lesson where the textbook image of glaciation at work is in fact laid out in front of you. From Red Tarn you have two ridges, both dramatic and sharp looking arêtes either side. This great combe was formed by a mass of ice that over time just gouged the whole lot out.

High Spying How is the rock tower, which marks the high point at the start of Striding Edge. From this point, weather permitting, you will see the whole of the Edge just stretching out in front. But as Wainwright didn't have the weather quite on his side this landmark took on gruesome proportions. 'We went on, heads down against the driving rain until, quite suddenly, a window opened in the mist ahead, disclosing a black tower of rock streaming with water, an evil and

Helvellyn from Red Tarn

threatening monster that stopped us in our tracks. Then the mist closed in again and the apparition vanished. We were scared: there were unseen terrors ahead.'

Not just because of AW's slightly menacing descriptions, but also because of the slightly exposed nature of ridge walking, tackling Striding Edge felt like a challenge. As AW very succinctly states it is 'an airy rock ridge', but one that he also described as 'very fine indeed'. For those daunted by its airy proportions and vertiginous aspect be also reassured that Wainwright added that it has a 'good path throughout'. If your heart is in your mouth, slow and steady progress seems to be the best remedy. I'm not always the greatest fan of that slightly exposed feeling of loftiness but there's plenty to concentrate on as you make your way across the Edge. Just keeping a watchful eye on where you place your feet and hands can feel like a welcome enough distraction.

Wainwright's first expedition up here certainly sounded dramatic: 'We were on Striding Edge...a platform of naked rock that vanished into the mist as a narrow ridge with appalling precipices on both sides. In agonies of apprehension, we edged our way along the spine of the ridge.'

A memorial en route gives further stark warning of the potential dangers of this dramatic ridge walk. Robert Dixon left his home in Patterdale on 27 November 1858 to follow the foxhound hunt. He was from a Lakeland hunting family but tragically that morning he fell from Striding Edge and plummeted to his untimely death. You will find his cast iron memorial sited on a level area overlooking Nethermost Cove. The inscription reads: 'In memory of Robert Dixon of Rooking Patterdale who was killed on this place on the 27th day of Nov 1856 following the Patterdale foxhounds'.

Striding Edge fully deserves its place as a Lakeland classic, revered and favoured by those who venture along it. On a clear day you can appreciate 300 yards (274 metres) of exposed narrow ridge.

Striding Edge

An aerial view of the final approach to Helvellyn's summit, a 300-foot (91-metre) face of steep rock and loose scree

Once on, there's no escape, save for going forwards or backwards. Yet for walkers with a reasonable head for heights and for those not pre-occupied with foxhunting, it is a very attainable and satisfying mountaineering achievement.

There is a little sting in the tail, just something to round off the experience nicely. What you will find at the very end is a sort of chimney that you can descend, much like coming backward down a ladder. Wainwright was perhaps a little wearier and weather battered than even the film crew and I, when he discovered this final challenging spot: 'After an age of anxiety we reached the abrupt end of the Edge and descended an awkward crack in the rocks to firmer ground below and beyond, feeling and looking like old men.

My cousin, looking like something fished from the sea, kept looking at me and saying nothing but was obviously

The summit, from Striding Edge

inwardly blaming me, as author of the day's programme, for his present misery.'

The final approach to Helvellyn's summit is a 300-foot (91-metre) face of steep rock and loose scree. Where Striding Edge tested your nerves, this will offer one final test to your fitness and stamina. Not bad for a 'little' climb. If you are blessed with slightly better conditions than I was, then somewhere up here, just where the climb meets the plateau, is another monument.

The Gough Memorial

Erected 1890 on the edge of the summit above the path to Striding Edge.

One of the best-known stories in the Lakes concerns a young artist who climbed this route 200 years ago. Charles Gough set off from Patterdale with his faithful Irish Terrier, 'Foxie'. Tragically three months later his shattered remains were found by a local shepherd. Gough had perished on the cliffs below, but there standing guard over his master's body, was Gough's dog, an event Wordsworth later chose to immortalize in a poem titled 'Fidelity' and Sir Walter Scott wrote about in his poem 'Helvellyn'.

From the memorial there's just a simple walk across the plateau to the summit, the largest, flattest peak of any of the Lake District giants. There's so much room that two daredevils even managed to land a plane here in 1926. This is where the hordes converge from all directions on a good day, quickening their pace as they spot the summit shelter. AW notes: 'There are few days in any year when no visitor calls at the wall shelter on the summit to eat his sandwiches.' It doesn't matter which way the wind's blowing, you'll find shelter there with protection on every side (definitely as good a butty stop as any I've discovered on a fell top).

But as AW notes the actual summit is perhaps not quite what you might have in mind: 'It might be expected that the summit of so popular a mountain would be crowned with a cairn the size of a house, instead of which the only adornment is a small and insignificant heap of stones that commands no respect at all.'

The summit spot may not have the most impressive cairn but it's the views which command attention, spectacular and extensive in every direction. To the north you might spy Blencathra and then Skiddaw to its side. There are also the great northwestern fells and on a good day you might even been able to see as far as Morecambe Bay.

Finally standing on Helvellyn's summit I was reminded of AW's description of Helvellyn as a 'friendly giant'. 'There is some quality about Helvellyn, which endears it in the memory

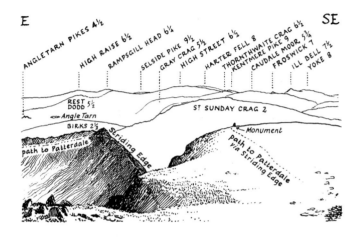

of most people who have stood on its breezy top; although it can be a grim place indeed on a wild night, it is as a rule a very friendly giant. If it did not inspire affection would its devotees return so often?'

Standing on Helvellyn for me certainly felt like a big tick and one of the great achievements in fellwalking. If you stay in any B&B in this area, somebody some day will ask you 'have you done Helvellyn and Striding Edge?' Of course, now I can say 'Yes'. Because I didn't have the very best conditions or always the clearest of views however, so the pull of Helvellyn is still there. I am now one of those devotees looking for the chance to return to this 'friendly giant'.

Julia sizes up the Helvellyn route, with Ullswater in the foreground

Julia's tips for a tipple:

The King's Head, (Thirlmere near Keswick) although more hotel than pub is very quirky, full of character, and definitely one to leave your boots outside of.
The White Lion (Patterdale) has pork scratchings, scampi and chips and a juke box. Good stuff.

CATBELLS

Julia's Overview

It was a blue-sky day, the perfect Lakeland offering. A light breeze shuffled the odd wave across the lake and the day felt full of promise. The sleeping town of Keswick was slowly beginning to wake to the possibilities that a fine weather day in the Lakes can bring. It was this tantalizing sense of possibility which greeted me at the foot of the delightfully named Catbells.

Here was a fell that was practically in Keswick's back garden, one that might easily be summited by young and old alike in a morning or afternoon. I couldn't think of any other fell that I had walked with quite such ease of access.

For a television crew staying in Keswick this walk was a dream location. We were tidily tucked away at the newly opened Oakthwaite B&B run by Karen and David. All you need to know is that David is a delightfully amenable former geography teacher – very organised (WiFi sorted) and Karen bakes the kind of cakes that you would push small children out of the way to scoff. (On many occasions we would return late afternoon, soaked and cold to the cartilage to her outstanding double chocolate fudge cake and pots of tea. Food, especially sweet chocolate-based food, is a big motivator for me). So we left the B&B on a Thursday morning with full tummies and the bounce that only a reasonable start time can give you (anything after 9am in my case).

After our Derwentwater boat crossing we began the easy ascent up the path. I stopped to deliver the PTC about Sir John Woodford, and took my jacket out of my backpack. As I finished delivering my words I walked past the camera,

The distinctive profile of Catbells
Pages 108-109: Catbells and Derwentwater

attempting to put the coat on as I left the shot. Regrettably a high wind whisked the item right into my face where it stayed slapped across my jowls like a wet tea towel 'smooth Miss Bradbury, smooth' muttered the team.

AW unforgettably describes Catbells as 'bold' with a 'come hither look.' It's a reminder of the fullness of AW's love affair with these rolling fells of Cumbria. His finely tuned descriptions were the carefully composed notes of an enthralled suitor to the subject he spent decades persuing. Will anyone ever be able to catch up...?

CATBELLS

· ·

ASCENT FROM HAWSE END
1250 feet of ascent : 1½ miles

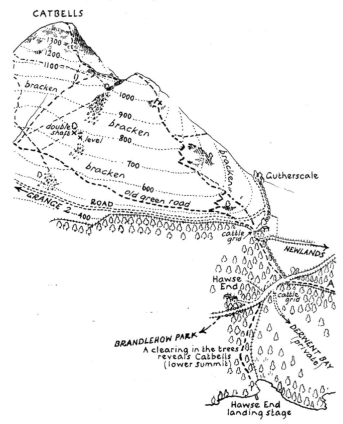

CATBELLS

1300
1200
1100

bracken

1000

900

bracken
800

double
shaft
level

700

bracken

600

old green road

ROAD

GRANGE 2

400

Gutherscale

cattle grid

NEWLANDS

Hawse End

cattle grid

DERWENT BAY (private)

BRANDLEHOW PARK

A clearing in the trees
reveals Catbells
(lower summit)

Hawse End
landing stage

THE WALK
Catbells — from Hawse End

SUMMIT HEIGHT: 1,481 feet/451 metres
(1,250 feet/381 metres of ascent)
DISTANCE: 1½ miles/2.4 kilometres
OS MAP: OL4
Pictorial Guide Book Six – The North Western Fells

'Its ascent from Keswick may conveniently in the holiday season be coupled with a sail on the lake, making the expedition rewarding out of all proportion to the small effort needed. Even the name has a magic challenge to it.'
A. Wainwright

OVERVIEW
Heeding AW's advice I chose to take my walk in the 'holiday season' when my stomp could be combined with a truly picturesque 'sail' across Derwentwater. Stepping aboard one of the traditional wooden launches, which plough a route across its outstretched waters, you pass a number of the picture postcard islands, which dot this beautiful lake. But it's not too long before you are delivered to the western shores and the lakeside jetty at Hawse End where the walk begins in earnest. The route initially heads off through woodland before reaching the foot of Catbells. The path then splits in two. This walk follows the route up the north breast of the fell, taking the engineered zigzags. The path is then interrupted by a short scramble up a polished rock face, before reaching a stony plateau. From here, you walk along the top of the distinctive steady ridge, which gives Catbells its famous profile. It has three distinct impressions before reaching a heavily eroded tower of rock, which leads to a steepish climb and the rugged and exposed summit.

The Walk

'Words cannot adequately describe the rare charm of Catbells, nor its ravishing view, but no publicity is necessary, its mere presence in the Derwentwater scene is enough.'
A. Wainwright

The view west over Derwentwater in winter (Catbells is in the left of the frame)

Bustling Keswick is the start-point for this walk, or rather the shores of AW's lovely 'Derwentwater scene'. Head down to the lakeshore and you will see how Catbells beckons, crowning the panorama with its shapely curves, drawing walkers time and time again to make the journey by boat to reach its foot at Hawse End. Rising as gracefully as it does in the heart of such Lakeland majesty it's no surprise to find that Catbells is indeed one of the most photographed viewpoints in the whole of the Lake District. Its 'shapely topknot' as well as those 'smooth, sunny and sleek' slopes continue to hold the eye for today's wanderers, walkers and visitors, just as they caught Wainwright's gaze.

Now, the one thing that everybody seems to know about Wainwright is that he liked to walk alone. He didn't like to be disturbed or approached on his walks, he wanted to focus all his energies on getting every detail just right for his books. But Catbells was the one walk where he actively encouraged families to follow in his footsteps. He describes it as 'a family fell where grandmothers and infants can climb the heights together'. As soon as you step out on this walk you begin to sense just how much today's walkers, of all generations, have taken this advice. For some 'little'uns' it may well be their first taste of the fells and the spectacle of families slowly trundling upwards will become a familiar and cheering sight on this walk.

After making your way up from the landing stage through the lovely cloaking woodland there are two paths, both marked in the guide, but Wainwright states that the zigzag route is 'exquisite' and a 'more enjoyable start to the ascent' (well, I'm not one to ignore AW's recommendations, so zigzags it was for me).

An aerial view of Woodford's engineered zigzag path

This specially laid out route is known as 'Woodford's Path' after its creator Sir John Woodford. He was an army Major General and veteran of Waterloo who had a summer home at Derwent Bay near the jetty. He used his experience of digging trenches and making defences to engineer this impressive path purely to use on excursions from his home. Now, more than a hundred and thirty years later it has become much more than the route for one man's private wanderings. Wainwright even describes it as an 'enchanting stairway'.

As you reach just under 1,000 feet (308 metres) you will start to see some of the more visible signs of all these visitors. Countless walkers have passed over this rocky ground, so many that the surface here has become really polished and you may even need to get your hands a bit dirty with some gentle scrambling over this slightly more uneven section. If you can, stop for a moment and look out for the plaque dedicated to Thomas Arthur Leonard. It is after all Mr Leonard we may wish to thank for some of our outdoor freedoms today. One of the key instigators of the 'The Open Air Movement', Leonard is also known as the 'father of hiking' and was responsible for getting the Ramblers' Association underway in 1891. He pioneered country holidays for families from the industrial centres of nineteenth century Britain, families from similar backgrounds to Wainwright's own humble working class origins in Blackburn.

After this brief stop off it's not too long before you will be rewarded with your first view of the summit. What makes this walk so distinctive is its sheer accessibility. You can be so close to all the creature comforts of Keswick and yet within about half an hour, you get a viewpoint like this. In one direction there is an unfolding vista across Derwentwater to Blencathra, or Saddleback as it is sometimes known. Standing behind Keswick is the giant peak of Skiddaw and looking north towards Bassenthwaite Lake, the valley looks straight down to the Solway Firth and the Scottish hills beyond. As Wainwright all too finely puts it, this is one 'ravishing view'.

There is something altogether magical about this fell. Striding out along its gentle contours you also step into a world of storytelling and folklore. You need only look back down the lake to pick out the northwestern shores of Derwentwater. Nestled here is Fawe Park where Beatrix Potter spent one summer holidaying in July 1903. It was a visit that would later inspire The Tale of Benjamin Bunny and many of the book's garden illustrations were versions of its grounds. Looking back down on the lake you can also spy Herbert's Island; supposedly the nut-gathering haunt of Potter's other much loved character, Squirrel Nutkin. Over to the west, peek into Newlands Valley where you'll find Little Town and the home of a certain legendary washerwoman hedgehog, Mrs Tiggywinkle, who supposedly lived close-by.

This is an area which seems to have inspired the

Julia strides out above the Newlands Valley, the supposed home of Beatrix Potter's much loved Mrs Tiggywinkle
Right: An aerial view of Catbell's summit

imagination. For today's walker some of the allure lies, as Wainwright states, in the name. 'Catbells' just seems to have something of the fairy-tale about it, or as AW put it 'a magic challenge'. But its meaning also has people divided. Wainwright commits to one view stating it might well be a corruption of 'Cat *Bields*,' which means 'the shelter of the wild cat', although AW also notes this this has been disputed by 'authorities of repute'.

As you steadily progress upwards the views certainly reward, from almost every angle. 'Scenes of great beauty unfold on all sides and they are scenes in depth to a degree not usual,' wrote AW, adding 'it is to Derwentwater and mid-Borrowdale that the captivated gaze returns again and again.'

As resplendent as the views are there are also some visible scars on this landscape. Wainwright in fact warns: 'This fell is not quite so innocuous as is usually thought, and grandmothers and infants should take care as they

romp around.' Once home to a booming mining industry AW takes great pains to highlight the perils of some of the open shafts 'that pierce the fell on both flanks' and even goes as far as to fastidiously draw some of the old workings, reminding the reader of 'a tragic death' in one in 1962. But the unsuspecting walker could easily miss some of the more surprising industrial history of this fell, as it remains buried beneath its very summit.

There are a number of mines beneath your feet, in fact about four different veins actually course through the fell. Lower down there is Old Brandley, and then further on Brandlehow. But the largest mine on the fell is actually right under the top of Catbells. As you stand aloft the summit it may come as a surprise to find that right below you is Yewthwaite Mine and around about 1,000 feet (304.8 metres) of mineshaft.

A dangerous hole at Yewthwaite Mine.

Julia looks down into Newlands Valley

Intriguingly it was Germans who first mined here, brought over by Queen Elizabeth I. They were considered to be the leading lights in mining copper and lead with far greater expertise because they had the ability to not only dig and prospect, but also to smelt the ore. In fact they built the biggest smelt mill in Europe, just over in Keswick at Brigham.

When you walk across the fells you see hints of the mining industry that was, but you'd perhaps never know that it was so prolific. A staggering fifty to seventy thousand tonnes of lead was mined here in the 1850s and subsequently twenty different commercial mines, which over the last 400 years have created fabulous wealth and employment. In 1900 half the local male population was working in mining. But today's fells have an altogether different sort of business. Perhaps there is no better spot in the Lakes, which shows how the old industry of mining has been replaced by the new industry of tourism. Where once we'd have been looking at the filthy miners trudging their way up to the various shafts and workings, we now see similar hordes of people winding their way upwards for the sheer pleasure of being in this outdoor landscape.

With all this mention of accessibility and talk of the family fell you might think this would be a crowded walk. But it seems to me that a quiet moment can always be found in the fells and as Wainwright all too finely puts 'silence is always more profound in places where there was once noise.'

Once you find a quiet moment in the fells it can sometimes be hard to drag yourself onwards but the final stretch takes you upwards and onto the final spine of the walk. The path along this ridge is straight and uncomplicated and you continue to have fantastic views of the valleys on one side whilst also looking out across the water on the other. Looking straight ahead from here the path just goes all the way to the summit, your final goal in sight, which for little legs and older legs may well be a welcome goal to fix on.

The summit cone is reached by a final rocky stairway, which is heavily eroded, almost mirroring the internal scars of this old industrial landscape. As you get closer to the top, you begin to understand what Wainwright meant when he said it isn't as innocuous as it first looks.

One last scramble for the top delivers you onto a surprising summit. I thought it would be grassy, instead it's actually rugged rock underfoot and it's small, perhaps even the smallest summit I've been on. But with that small summit comes incredibly big and bold views.

Wainwright described the scene: 'The summit, which has no cairn, is a small platform of naked rock, light brown in colour and seamed and pitted with many tiny hollows

Catbells Pinnacle
No ropes, pitons, etriers and other gadgets are needed to conquer this fine rock monolith.
(It is only four feet high)

and crevices that collect and hold rainwater – so that, long after the skies have cleared, glittering diamonds adorn the crown. Almost all of the native vegetation has been scoured away by the varied footgear of countless visitors that often it is difficult to find a vacant perch. In the summer it is not a place to seek quietness'.

It's a very different sense of achievement from conquering one of the big Lakeland fells. You can get to the top of Catbells in under an hour, or it can be the pinnacle of a grand family day out, either way when you are here you get the full flavour of the Lake District.

The joy of Catbells is in its accessibility, a simple fell that offers it all. There's the bustle of starting in a town, a sail across the lake, consistently impressive views, teamed with the temptation of distant dramatic panoramas; a great walk, and an occasional scramble. Catbells has been a favourite in Keswick since the dawn of fellwalking and today it's easy to see why Wainwright's simple description still rings true. This really is a 'truly lovely walk'.

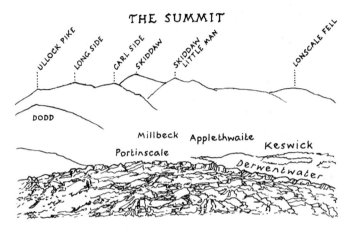

THE SUMMIT

ULLOCK PIKE LONG SIDE CARL SIDE SKIDDAW SKIDDAW LITTLE MAN LONSCALE FELL

DODD

Millbeck Applethwaite Keswick

Portinscale

Derwentwater

Julia's tips for a tipple:

There are two tearooms in Grange which are the closest establishments but for that pint there's The Farmers' Arms or The Derwentwater Hotel (Portinscale).

CRINKLE CRAGS & BOWFELL

Julia's Overview

There's really no such thing as just another Wainwright walk. There is nothing ordinary or mundane about his routes, each one always delivers a special moment, a certain glimpse of a hidden vista or an unimagined view. Our day on Crinkle Crags and Bowfell looked to be no different because stretching out ahead was the longest Wainwright route we'd tackled for the series.

Our programme budgets are small (we could film ten, maybe fifteen walks for every episode of *Top Gear*) and time is very precious. When you only have one day to film, every shot counts. Rain and adverse weather slow the process down, presenters can slow the process down, nervous interviewees can slow things down and laughter can really get in the way. 6½ miles to cover with nothing but a sandwich stop is a cinch but when you're filming everything pretty along the way it's a different story.

Wainwright declared his love for Bowfell early on, openly listing it in Book Four as one of the best half-dozen. Great Langdale is one of the best known and most-visited valleys in the Lake District, a spot where walking and camping sit happily beside the ongoing traditions of upland farming. Around these neatly walled fields, visitors like me come to explore streams, screes, lonely tarns and hidden waterfalls. Standing, watching over the very head of the valley, are Bowfell and Crinkle Crags.

It wasn't just the need to conquer both peaks in one day that was attractive (two for the price of one), it was also a walk that allowed me to understand how the mind of the

An aerial view of the Langdale Valley
Pages 124-125: Bowfell and Crinkle Crags from Long Top

great man worked and experience first hand why he was such an ardent fan of the ridge walk. He wrote that 'Ridges, in general, provide the best fellwalking in Lakeland... they are the high-level traverses that link mountain summits and invariably reward the walker with ever-changing, distant panoramas and aerial views of ethereal beauty.... Ridgewalking is fellwalking at its best.' and this walk offered 'Lakeland's best ridge-mile'. No pressure to capture all that on camera then...in one day.

CRINKLE CRAGS & BOWFELL

. . . .

ASCENT FROM DUNGEON GHYLL (via RED TARN)
2600 feet of ascent : 4 miles

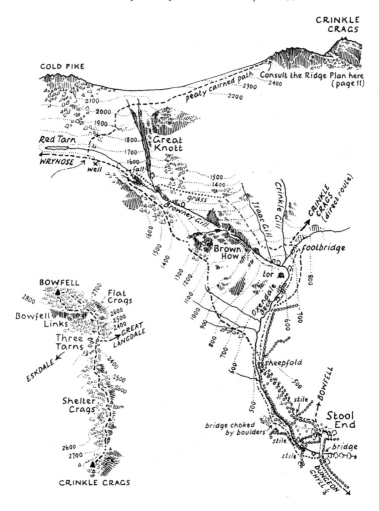

CRINKLE
CRAGS

COLD PIKE

Consult the Ridge Plan here
(page 11)

peaty cairned path

2300
2400
2200

2100
2000
1900
1800
1700
1600

Red Tarn

WRYNOSE

well

fall

Great
Knott

1500
1400

grass

Isaac Gill

Crinkle Gill

CRINKLE
CRAGS
(direct route)

footbridge

Browney Gill

1600

1500

1400

1300

1200

1100

Brown
How

tor

Oxendale

800

BOWFELL

2800

Bowfell
Links

Three
Tarns

ESKDALE

2700

Flat
Crags

2600
2500
2400

GREAT
LANGDALE

2400

2500
2600

Shelter
Crags

tarn

2600
2700

CRINKLE CRAGS

1000

900

800

700

600

700

sheepfold

500

stile

600

500

bridge choked
by boulders

stile

stile

BOWFELL

Stool
End

bridge

DUNGEON
GHYLL

THE WALK
Crinkle Crags & Bowfell – from Great Langdale
(ascent from Dungeon Ghyll via Red Tarn)

SUMMIT HEIGHT:
Crinkle Crags: 2,816 feet/859 metres – Bowfell: 2,960 feet/902 metres
(3,950 feet/1,203 metres of ascent)
DISTANCE: 6.5 miles/10.4 kilometres
OS MAP: OL 6
Pictorial Guide Book Four – The Southern Fells

'Crinkle Crags is much too good to be missed. For the
mountaineer who prefers his mountains rough...
this is a climb deserving of high priority.'
'Bowfell is a mountain of noble aspect and rare
distinction... It is a challenge that cannot be denied.'
A. Wainwright

OVERVIEW

Sitting on its very own at the top end of Great Langdale is Stool End
Farm, the last outpost of civilization on this walk. Pass through and the
route heads up Oxendale, crossing the beck, before taking a long and
steady climb beside the ravine of Browney Gill. Eventually you emerge
onto flatter ground at Red Tarn. This is a turning point as you move
northwest across a great expanse of peaty grassland. The gentle path
gives way as you approach the many rugged peaks of Crinkle Crags.
This is where Wainwright's ultimate ridge walk begins, delivering a
mile of classic views and fell-top scrambling. The pass of Three Tarns
nestles between Crinkle Crags and Bowfell. From here, I chose to make
my way across to the Climbers' Traverse. This path takes you into a
world of towering cliffs and shattered rock, including the unmistakeable
feature known simply as the Great Slab. From here, it's just a short
climb across rocks to one of the most shapely summit peaks in the
whole of Lakeland.

The Walk

'...its lofty serrated ridge, a succession of knobs
and depressions, is aptly described by the
name. These undulations, seeming trivial from a
distance, are revealed at close range as steep
buttresses and gullies above wild declivities,
a scene of desolation and rugged grandeur
equalled by few others in the district.'
A. Wainwright

*An aerial view of Crinkle Crags and Bowfell with Stool End Farm in the
foreground*

This walk definitely felt like a big day out when I started. I had my plan; tackling Crinkle Crags first by approaching from the south, before making my way along the entire ridge to the summit of Bowfell. But this is over a mile of the most exposed land in the Lakes and as we all know, walking in the fells, is never predictable.

So, it was with both brimming anticipation and also just a bit of trepidation that I made my way to Stool End Farm, which is a working uplands farm but also a major thoroughfare for fellwalkers arriving in and leaving from Great Langdale.

After the farm buildings the soft Lakeland environment becomes much wilder. The nearby riverbed of Oxendale is strewn with massive boulders. Just looking at the mess of rocks, which line its sides, you can begin to imagine some of the raging weather and rumbling storms this valley sees, when water levels rise and these boulders are pushed down, like little pebbles, by the force of the water.

Once you reach the footbridge the walk takes a sudden turn upwards and the path leaves Oxendale and heads south up a gully destined for Red Tarn. This the first proper climb of the day, (in fact it's the most intense piece of ascent of the whole route). My advice is simple, just take it nice and steady, or this can feel like a relentless slog up 1,100 feet (335 metres). The path skirts a ravine that gets progressively more dramatic as you climb. This is Browney Gill, cut over the millennia since the last Ice Age and now a small oasis of rowan trees and flowering plants.

Few big fellwalks are complete without a trip to a tarn and this route is certainly no exception. Red Tarn is the first of this route, a 'walkers' crossroads' as Wainwright described

Great Langdale at sunrise from the band path to Bowfell

it, with four paths converging where the stream exits the lake. This isn't the most picturesque tarn I've visited. It seems to be just parked in the middle of this very open pass, utterly exposed to the elements. But that aside, it is still a good goal to aim for as you slog up Browney Gill and the view from it right across to Bowfell is magic. Wainwright described Red Tarn as 'an unattractive sheet of water' but did concede that it might have its uses on a hot day. With a great deal still to tick-off I didn't have time to consider a paddle during my walk (or really the inclination. It looked pretty cold).

The good news is that much of the hard graft of ascent has now been done. The walk from here on changes its character. The route to the first of the Crinkle Crags brings you onto an inspiring high fell plateau. This is where the air changes, the wind changes and views open up as you stride across the gentlest of gradients. In the distance behind you grand vistas reveal Lake Windermere at the end of the Langdale Valley.

As you start to walk across this grassy plain, for about a mile you can loose a bit of the drama that lies ahead. Then, the Crinkles reveal themselves. The gentle path across the grass gives way to boulders and scrambling as you approach this most distinctive of fell tops. It's as you scale the first of the five mini summits that you get a clear view of the second and highest Crinkle at 2,818 feet (859 metres). But in the way stands the largest obstacle on any footpath in Lakeland.

The ominously named 'Bad Step' looks exactly like Wainwright's drawing. 'Chicken hearted walkers, muttering something about discretion being the better part of valour, will sneak away and circumvent the difficulty by following the author's footsteps around the flank of the buttress... Two chockstones block the gully entirely, forming a rocky wall ten feet high, quite beyond the powers of the average walker to scale.'

The Bad Step
from below

From my own experience of this rocky conundrum, the 'Bad Step', is largely a problem solving exercise. Once you realise you'd have to be 8 feet tall to climb straight over the chockstones it then becomes a case of choosing which bit of sidewall to climb. As Wainwright warns 'The Bad Step is the most difficult obstacle met on any of the regular walkers' paths in Lakeland' so it certainly needs to be tackled with a cool head and some flexibility (both in mind and body). A combination of hands, feet and the odd knee should then see you through.

From here it's just a few yards over rocks to reach the true summit of Crinkle Crags, where a stunning vista opens out in front of you. There's Langdale all the way down to the right. Eskdale on the left and then the magnificent Scafell range in a big horseshoe out in front. But look north and you will see in sharp focus what's to come and where you're headed as Bowfell rises resplendent. No wonder Wainwright thought this was the best ridge-mile walk in the whole of Lakeland.

From here the ridge walk begins in earnest and the route

The fourth and fifth Crinkles (Shelter Crags and Bowfell behind), seen from the third Crinkle

Julia takes a break beside the Three Tarns

falls and rises as you traverse the rest of Crinkle Crags. A little scramble to the top of Crinkle Three is a minor diversion but your reward is a terrific view of Great Langdale, down and through the valley. I think these detours are really worth it, not just for the view but because they help you to get the true lie of the land. This fine ridge once included the local county boundary. When Wainwright published his *Pictorial Guides*, this was where Cumberland and Westmorland ran alongside each other, both now consigned to the history books, in favour of the modern day Cumbria.

Bowfell from this angle really is quite a sight. It's a great pyramid of a mountain. I don't think the word 'fell' really describes it adequately, at a whopping 2,959 feet (902 metres) this really is a mountain. As AW puts it, this is the heart of 'Lakeland's best ridge-mile' and he certainly gave it the attention it deserves. In fact he presented it in a level of detail that was unique, even for him. He dedicated a

THE SUMMIT

staggering twenty pages to his description of Crinkle Crags and a further twenty pages to Bowfell. There is a plan of the entire ridge from Red Tarn along the Crinkles which is full of lovely, carefully observed detail, as you'd expect from Wainwright. But supposing you were coming in the opposite direction from the Three Tarns, you'd think you would just have to turn the book around. Not with Wainwright. Such was his obsession and attention to every detail he did it for you, exactly the same route but the other way round. Now that's what I call service.

After a mile of fairly intense rocky scrambling you may find it quite a relief to be heading downwards towards gentler, grassier ground. It's a welcome chance to take the pressure off your knees as you approach the ideal rest spot at Three Tarns.

This is the most popular pass-route between the mighty valleys of Langdale and Eskdale. The three tarns themselves are so small they can be easily missed and depending on the weather, you may only find two tarns, or even as many as four. Either way, this is where we leave Wainwright's Crinkle Crags chapter and turn attention to the second mountain of the day.

An aerial view of the Great Slab

Bowfell

'Bowfell is a mountain that commands attention whenever it appears in a view. And more than attention, respect and admiration, too; for it has the rare characteristic of displaying a graceful outline and a sturdy shapeliness on all sides.'
A. Wainwright

The next challenge is to navigate off the main route from Three Tarns and find the Climbers' Traverse, the path that Wainwright thought showed Bowfell at its very best. The Climbers' Traverse isn't a public right of way, so it doesn't appear on the OS Map but once you find it there is a path that takes you off the ridge. It has one or two moments where you have to slither around, but the only real difficulty comes once you reach the bottom of Bowfell buttress.

The only way is up and there is quite a nasty looking scree slope. Its difficulty is however more to do with exertion than anything technical, so be sure to leave some fuel in the engine for the end of the day and the final push to the summit.

The Great Slab of Flat Crags

Now the name might suggest that harnesses and hand-holds are required but fortunately the Climbers' Traverse isn't quite that dramatic. The path first developed to provide access straight to the favoured spots of rock-climbers. It follows a ledge that passes round the great supporting walls of Bowfell. This is where climbers come to tackle Flat Crags, Cambridge Crags and the suitably named Bowfell Buttress.

Walkers who stick to the main route from Three Tarns can easily spend an entire day on Bowfell without ever noticing the drama that sits under their noses. But from this angle on the Climbers' Traverse the summit sort of grows out of a riverbed of scree stones and juts up into the sky.

Thankfully AW doesn't recommend going up the scree to approach the summit. You are left instead with an unlikely climb up the side of Cambridge Crag and a route past the most unusual feature of the day. In amongst all the near vertical rock faces, is one very different one, Great Slab, as Wainwright called it, a vast and gently sloping platform of naked rock. Uniquely this unmistakable landmark somehow

stands aloof of the scree surrounding it.

A 'gushing waterspout' at the base of Cambridge Cliffs provides another landmark. You might well fancy a sip of its icy fresh water. This lovely ice cold refreshment is certainly a good way to prepare for the final climb of this Lakeland epic and as Wainwright put it 'Nothing better ever came out of a barrel or a bottle'. (And what a place to stop, you're surrounded by some of the boldest mountain features in the country).

Wainwright was so impressed with the Great Slab and the Langdale Pikes in the distance that he even gave it a double page spread. As you round the top of Great Slab, the summit of Bowfell is both unmistakeable and reassuringly close. It's an exciting summit that really keeps the challenge, as well as the drama, going right to the very end. Wainwright describes Bowfell's top as 'a shattered pyramid, a great heap of stones

An aerial view of walkers on Bowfell summit

and boulders and naked rock, a giant cairn in itself.'

There really is no doubting when you're at the very top. No need for a triangulation point or a great summit cairn (I'm not quite sure where you'd build one anyway). It is certainly a summit that delivers a dramatic punch with its craggy rock hewn formations. As AW so rightly states 'these crags are of diverse and unusual form, natural curiosities that add an exceptional interest and help to identify Bowfell in the memory.'

Getting to this spot does feel like a big achievement, a major tick on the Wainwright list. Carefully picking your way up here is definitely worth the effort entailed, it really does deliver something you can only discover by pulling on your boots and walking. As AW explained simply it's a summit which 'reserves its best rewards for the walkers who climb the natural rocky stairway to its upper limit for here, spread before them for their delection, is a glorious panorama.'

Throughout seven whole volumes, this was the only fell Wainwright admitted straight away, was 'among the best half-dozen... a summit deserving of detailed exploration and rewarding visitors with very beautiful views.' He loved to bestow honours, and create a rankings system that would inspire endless debate on footpaths and in pubs across the Lakes, but every other fell had to wait until he published his final *Pictorial Guide* to learn whether they would join Bowfell in Wainwright's premier league.

In 1966 that final and much anticipated volume was published and Wainwright revealed Crinkle Crags to also be one of his six best. So, this really is a walk of true classics; two top fells, one monster expedition and between them a route, which can continue the debate Wainwright so plainly loved. Could this be the greatest ridgewalk in England? It certainly rates on my list.

Julia's tips for a tipple:

The Old Dungeon Ghyll (Langdale) has a great bar serving traditional ales. It's full of character, a real walkers' pub. The New Dungeon Ghyll is similar but slightly more genteel.

Julia's Overview

Helm Crag intrigued me right from the start. Situated in the very heart of the Lake District, it is one of the lowest summits in Book Three of Wainwright's *Pictorial Guides*. So I was curious to know just what it was about this fell that Wainwright loved so much, because rather surprisingly, this mini mountain had made it into AW's top six summits, despite being the only peak he never got to the very top of.

Wainwright complained that the Helm Crag fellwalk itself was too short; news that lifted my companions' spirits. My sister Gina, my nephew Jack along with Lotte (the family miniature schnauzer), and a friend affectionately known as Lucy Goose, had joined us for the expedition. The sun was golden and on full beam all day – perfect conditions. In the morning they were all smiles, gently chastising me about my 'tough job' and the 'horrible views'. That night when we made it back to the hotel I think it's fair to say that everyone was exhausted in a fulfilled, happy way. The following day there were fewer smiles, Lotte had to be carried everywhere and Goose couldn't move her thighs without extreme discomfort. When I popped my head around her bedroom door at 8am to see if she was coming with us she grimaced and rather less than politely told me to go away. 'How can you walk another step?' she asked. 'We've still got days and days of filming ahead of us! No choice' I smiled. She groaned. The job swap was off.

My walk also had some other unexpected surprises. I had the pleasure of meeting local broadcaster and writer, Mark Richards. As well being an ardent fan of this fell he'd had the great fortune of meeting and walking with AW. He is also a champion talker. Presumably if you're reading this book you're probably all too aware that I can talk the hind legs off a donkey but trust me when I say I'm an amateur compared to Mark.

With his charming rapid delivery Mark explained how he and AW had both shared a love of ink drawings and had been introduced through family friends. He also explained how well matched Wainwright and his second wife Betty were – describing her as 'dependable as an OS Map'. Not the most romantic of descriptions but you get the picture!

Mark was also the privileged owner of a gift from AW – a book that Wainwright had in turn been given when he left his job at Blackburn Borough Council. It was a sort of early travelogue following a grand tour through the Alps, full of beautiful ink drawings of the mountains. There was one sketch in particular, of a Victorian traveller opening up a little pocket guidebook and it was entitled, 'Consulting Murray'. I could well imagine AW looking at this book and thinking, 'Hmm, there's something here, this could be consulting Wainwright not Murray'. That little book could well have been one of the inspirations that set AW on his lifetime's mission.

So my visit to the mini-fell of Helm Crag promised some big things. I think when we set off we might just have left Mark still talking about some of those virtues….

Pages 142-143: Helm Crag summit

HELM CRAG

. . . .

ASCENT FROM GRASMERE
1100 feet of ascent : 1½ miles

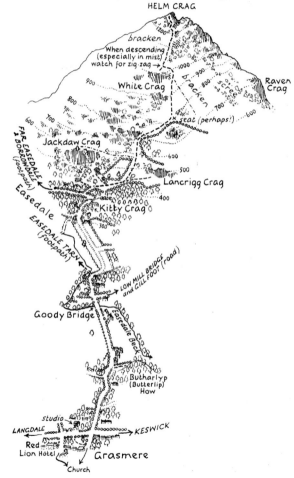

HELM CRAG

1200

bracken

When descending
(especially in mist)
watch for zig-zag →

1000

900

800

White Crag

900

bracken

800

700

Raven
Crag

600

scree

700

600

seat (perhaps!)

Jackdaw Crag

600

500

Lancrigg Crag

FAR EASEDALE
& BORROWDALE
(footpath)

Easedale

400

Kitty Crag

300

EASEDALE TARN
(footpath)

LOW MILL BRIDGE
and GILL FOOT (road)

Goody Bridge

Easedale Beck

Butharlyp
(Butterlip)
How

studio

LANGDALE

KESWICK

Red
Lion Hotel

Grasmere

Church

THE WALK
Helm Crag – from Grasmere

SUMMIT HEIGHT: 1,328 feet/405 metres
(1,100feet/335 metres of ascent)
DISTANCE: 1.5 miles/2.4 kilometres
OS MAP: OL7
Pictotial Guide Book Three – The Central Fells

'The virtues of Helm Crag have not been lauded
enough. It gives an exhilarating little climb,
a brief essay in real mountaineering, and, in
a region where all is beautiful, it makes a
notable contribution to the natural charms
and attractions of Grasmere.'
A. Wainwright

OVERVIEW

The walk begins in the heart of Grasmere village, although
you soon step away from the tourist crowds and towards the
western side of the fell crossing the National Trust estate at
Allan Bank. The route heads along the tarmaced Easedale
Road before heading into the woodland at the foot of Helm
Crag. An engineered rocky stairway then snakes its way up
the breast of the fell, passing by Lancrigg Crag, Jackdaw
Crag and White Crag. From the path there's a view across
Easedale Beck to Easedale Tarn and the spectacular waterfall
of Sour Milk Gill. The path then hairpins to the right, climbing
onto a ridge that gives a view into the opposite valley, looking
towards the pass of Dunmail Raise and the peak of Fairfield.
From here the final ascent leads to the summit ridge path
and the distinctive rocks that form the 'Lion and the Lamb'.
It then leads across the boulder strewn craggy and desolate
ridge top to reach the canon-shaped barrel of rock – 'The
Howitzer', which is the mountain's true top.

The Walk

'This is a splendid little climb; if it has a fault it is that it is too short. But for the evening of the day of arrival in Grasmere on a walking holiday it is just the thing: an epitome of Lakeland concentrated in the space of two hours- and an excellent foretaste of happy days to come.'
A. Wainwright

An aerial view of Helm Crag looking down over the village of Grasmere

It might sound like an odd suggestion for the start of a walk but it's sort of worth briefly detouring to the A591. From this buzzing highway you can actually catch a glimpse of your end goal and the very shapely formations that have earned Helm Crag its alternative name. Wainwright wrote: 'Generations of Wagonette and motor-coach tourists have been tutored to recognise its appearance in the Grasmere landscape: it is the one feature of their Lakeland tour they hail at sight and in unison, but the cry on their lips is not 'Helm Crag' but 'The Lion and the Lamb'.' From down on the roadside you can see exactly what Wainwright means.

Helm Crag is a modest 1,328 feet (405 metres), a fellwalk that is well known for being short and easy. As AW described it as a walk that was easily accomplished in a couple of hours I dutifully planned my walk as an early evening excursion, giving myself time in the late afternoon to explore Grasmere the popular Lakeland village from which the walk departs. This was also famously home to the eighteenth century poet William Wordsworth and his family.

Dove Cottage is Wordsworth's most famous residence and it now houses the Wordsworth Museum. But, a perhaps lesser-known house is Allan Bank, which you can spy from the walk once you leave the village behind and head along Easedale Road. This is where he lived with his wife Mary, their five children and his poet friend Samuel Coleridge between 1808–1811. In 1917 this impressive house gained another important owner. It was purchased by Canon Hardwick Rawnsley the co-founder of the National Trust, who later retired here. When he died in 1920, he left the estate to the Trust, who still manage it today.

Although when you set off on this part of the walk you can see the summit of Helm Crag, there is a fair bit of

William Wordsworth's grave in Grasmere

low-level walking to do before you reach the foot of the fell. In Wainwright's Book Three there is a tiny diagram, which shows Helm Crag in relation to Grasmere, and which Wainwright says 'is the smallest (and most accurate) map in the book.'

What we also know is that it's the smallest map in any of Wainwright's *Pictorial Guides* and I think it's the smallest map I've ever seen, it's the size of a stamp.

This is the smallest (and most accurate!) map in the book

Although Wainwright recommends a late start you could add an extra leg to your walk. A short detour from the route to Helm Crag takes you across the valley to the spectacular waterfall Sour Milk Gill and Easedale Tarn where you have a fine view of Helm Crag's profile.

Sauntering along the low-level section of this walk it's very easy to see why this area attracted its share of artists and writers and what sparked their creative juices. At the foot of Helm Crag is another grand house, Lancrigg where the Lakeland Poets, including Wordsworth and Coleridge, used to meet and socialise. As Wainwright did with his guides, Wordsworth immortalized the beauty of the Lakes in his poetry. He was often seen wandering in this valley and surrounding fells, dictating his poetry aloud to his sister Dorothy.

Shortly after passing Lancrigg the route starts to change again as you head into woodland and a canopy of trees blocks out the light. A signpost points ahead to Easdale Tarn whilst Helm Crag is off to the right where the path now appears to be gently heading upwards. The walk to Helm Crag also features in Wainwright's 192 mile Coast to Coast walk, from St Bees Head in the west, crossing three national parks, to Robin Hood's Bay in the east, which all goes to making this a well-trodden route. AW also recommends you return from your walk by the same course: 'This is one of the few hills where ascent and descent by the same route is recommended, an alternative route has nothing in its favour.'

The footpath is slightly altered from the route AW recommends in the original Book Three, as the path has been pitched and repaired by the National Trust. Although it's unlikely you'll go astray, it's a good reminder that you should carry an Ordnance Survey map.

When Wainwright started walking the OS maps were drawn to a much larger scale, so the detail wouldn't have been there. Helm Crag would have looked just like a little blob. The new scale of the OS maps doubled, liberating Wainwright's work. 'They fascinated me. The one-inch maps we had to be content with before suffered from an absence of detail: they were magnificent maps, magnificently drawn

An aerial view of the southwestern side of Helm Crag, featuring its engineered stairway, snaking up the fellside

and magnificently accurate, but on the rough country of Lakeland, where summits and crags and tarns and streams were bewilderingly crowded in small compass and where the ground was so steeply sculptured that the contours almost touched, there was simply not room on the one-inch maps to show every feature that a walker would encounter on his travels.'

One of those features worth keeping an eye out for lies across the valley to the southeast. On a clear day winking in the distance is Sour Milk Gill. Fed from the waters of Easdale Tarn this spectacular waterfall gets its name from its foaming waters, which resemble milk when it's being churned into butter.

At just under 1,300 feet and only a mile and a half in distance this fell is deceptively steep. It doesn't take too long for this walk to get the blood pumping but neither does it take long before the rewards begin to open up before you. Very soon, resplendent views over Grasmere emerge. In the right light its lake glistens and almost glows. There are some beautiful gentle walks around the water but if you fancy some of the tougher challenges that the Lake District has to offer, then Grasmere is perfectly placed to tackle Helvellyn, the Langdale Pikes and the Scafells.

The final stretch to the summit gets a little stonier underfoot. It certainly is surprisingly gnarled and weathered up here with rocky bluffs, intriguing crevices and nooks and crannies. AW's description of this landscape is suitably apt: 'The summit is altogether a rather weird and fantastic place, well worth not merely a visit but a detailed and leisurely exploration. Indeed the whole fell, although of small extent, is unusually interesting; its very appearance is challenging; its sides are steep, rough and craggy; its top bristles; it looks irascible, like a shaggy terrier in a company of sleek greyhounds, for all around are loftier and smoother fells, circling the pleasant vale of Grasmere out of which Helm Crag rises so abruptly.'

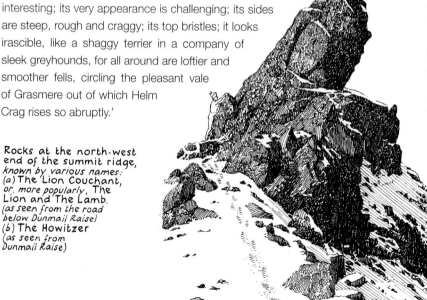

Rocks at the north-west end of the summit ridge, known by various names:
(a) The 'Lion Couchant, or, more popularly, The Lion and The Lamb, (as seen from the road below Dunmail Raise)
(b) The Howitzer (as seen from Dunmail Raise)

The distinctive rocky profile of the 'Lion and the Lamb'
Right: An aerial view of the final goal, the canon shaped barrel of rock,
'The Howitzer'

But once you actually make it up onto the top and find the rocky outcrops, which down on the roadside looked so clearly like a Lion and a Lamb, you can't actually make out their shape at all. Beneath you is the A591 and like me you will have become one of those little ant-like figures that you can see from down there, scuttling along the rocky profile.

Although this is a short walk and a low fell by Lakeland standards, it does make it into one of Wainwright's top six summits. When you look across this ridge, towards the other pinnacle of rock you can see why. 'The ridge path is a joy to tread and leads majestically to the main summit outcrop, a tilted jagged mass of rock which will draw a camera from any pack,' wrote AW.

The jagged mass of rock at the north of the summit is known as 'The Howitzer', and that's really the mountain's true top. This is one of the very few summits in Lakeland reached only by climbing rocks, Wainwright describes it as 'one of the very best'.

This looming top can certainly intimidate and to my mind looked like a much trickier proposition than I first imagined. So, the final inevitable challenge for me was to pitch myself against both the mountain and the man. I wanted to see if I could make the final scramble up this jutting piece of rock because of course AW never actually made it up there, although he was considerably older than I am when he tried.

Wainwright nevertheless still applauded the virtues of a trip up Helm Crag. He wrote: 'In scenic values the summits of many high mountains are a disappointment after the long toil of ascent, yet here, on top of little Helm Crag, a midget of a mountain, is a remarkable array of rocks, upstanding and fallen, of singular interest and fascinating appearance, that yield a quality of reward out of all proportion to the short and simple climb. The uppermost inches of Scafell and Helvellyn and Skiddaw can show nothing like Helm Crag's crown of shattered and petrified stone.'

The summit rocks from the north

Helm Crag from Grasmere

The whole feel of this walk from Grasmere to Helm Crag's summit is completely different from my other walks. Here the low-level journey to the foot of the fell makes a significant and enjoyable part of the route. The steep but relatively short hike up the fellside may deliver amazing views, but as Wainwright clearly realised, it is the rocky and desolate summit with its stark contrast to the valley below that delivers the walker the most inspiration and reward.

Wainwright reserved a little corner in Book Three in the Helm Crag section for an announcement that the author had succeeded in surmounting the highest point – which of course he never did. Sitting in the evening light on the summit of Helm Crag it's easy to see how this miniature fell winged its way into Wainwright's affections. Having scrambled to the top of this pinnacle of rock, I can tell you it's not as easy as it looks from down there in Grasmere. This might be a small fell but it certainly delivers a tricky final proposition. I think we can forgive AW for not making it to the very, very top.

Julia's tips for a tipple:

The Traveller's Rest Hotel, on the Grasmere road is where we ate after we finished filming the series and is a great walker's pub with meals.

Julia's Overview

Sandwiches and waterproofs; only two simple words but when you're walking every day for weeks at a time these two things become very important. No matter how gorgeous the day, no matter how bright the forecast, you pack your waterproofs. And you don't want the same sandwich filling darkening your Tupperware box every afternoon. I'm a terrible packer at the best of times and rarely travel light for the day or the fortnight. My backpack is full to the zip with spare clothes, including different tops, extra thermals (being of Greek descent I feel the cold), a spare pair of socks for the après stream crossing/puddle moment, chocolate, OS maps, mobile phone, ipod, water and make-up.

All I will say is I didn't pack enough for High Street. As we made our ascent to see the Roman road with our guest archaeologist Jamie Lund we got absolutely drenched. When we got to the top we couldn't see a thing due to the cloud. But despite this we stood strong and carried on. We pointed out various patches of cloud enthusiastically, under which lay the 'street' that had once existed as a busy thoroughfare. Luckily with the use of production archive and aerial shots, we were able to show the audience what we *should* have been looking at.

The endeavour of being outside and battling with the elements can be thoroughly exhilarating but is not great for filming. Sound equipment stops working, the lens gets fogged up and it takes at least twice as long to film everything. Getting soaked on a long hard walk can make you feel purposeful, strident and good about yourself. Getting wet through while you're trying to point things out on camera and impart information is just a pain. Never-the-less we ploughed on and allowed the surroundings to stir the imagination.

If you tackle High Street you'll find that what occurred here, going all the way back to Roman times, adds so much to this hike. You almost walk in step with the happenings and history of this valley and fell, propelled by past events that infuse an altogether more evocative atmosphere into the route. It's hard to put your finger on it. At times, these shadows of the past echo almost eerily, like at Haweswater Reservoir with its ghostly, submerged village. Whilst in other spots, like 'Racecourse Hill', you may well sense the mischief and merriment that others before you have enjoyed in these places. You may wish to heed Wainwright's well-worn advice and take the time, at some stage of your walk, to recline on the turf and witness this 'varied pageant of history, for he has been preceded here.'

We didn't recline in the turf on this occasion. The incessant rain had turned the 'turf' into soggy grassland. The waterproofs had ceased being waterproof hours before and my hair was doing a cunning impression of squid ink linguini clinging to my face. I can say in all honesty that when we achieved what was needed to complete the film we got down from High Street as fast as our cold, sodden limbs would carry us. A horse and carriage would have been most welcome that day...

Pages 158-159: High Street, the old Roman road across the summit ridge

HIGH STREET

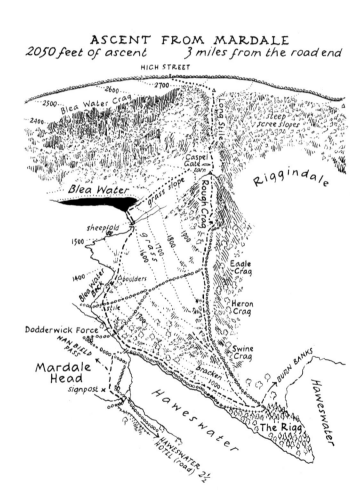

ASCENT FROM MARDALE
2050 feet of ascent   3 miles from the road end

HIGH STREET

2700
2600
2500 · Blea Water Crag
2400
Long Stile
steep
scree slopes
Caspel
Gate
tarn
Blea Water
grass slope
Riggindale
Rough Crag
sheepfold
1500
grass
1800
1900
1700
1600
1400
Eagle
Crag
Blea Water Beck
boulders
Heron
Crag
stile
1700
Dodderwick Force
Swine
Crag
NAN BIELD PASS
Mardale
Head
signpost ×
bracken
1000
BURN BANKS
Haweswater
Haweswater
The Rigg
HAWESWATER
HOTEL (road) 2½

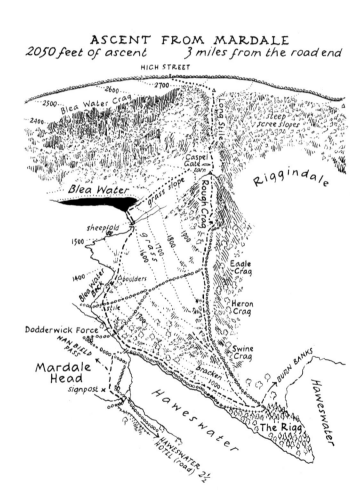

THE WALK
High Street – from Mardale

SUMMIT HEIGHT: 2,718 feet / 828 metres
(2,050 feet / 625 metres of ascent)
DISTANCE: 3 miles / 4.8 kilometres
OS MAP: OL5
Pictorial Guide Book Two – The Far Eastern Fells

'The ridge of Rough Crag and the rocky stairway of Long Stile together form the connoisseur's route up High Street, the only route that discloses the finer characteristics of the fell.'
A. Wainwright

OVERVIEW

The walk begins from the car park at the southern end of Haweswater Reservoir initially following the lakeshore, before reaching the conifer plantation at the promontory named 'The Rigg'. The path now strikes up a well-defined ridge passing the summits of Heron Crag, Swine Crag, Eagle Crag and Rough Crags. From the ridge the view looks into Blea Water Crag and down upon Blea Water Tarn, with the lesser tarn of Small Water beyond it to the south. The ridge narrows into a steep and rocky staircase called 'Long Stile'. This brings you to a small cairn where the ridge is met by the plateau. A grassy path leads across a vast plateau, heading towards an old triangulation column and a huge open vista that is the summit's true top. The indistinct route of the Roman road lies here between the two visible paths.

The Walk

'Most of the high places in Lakeland have no mention
in history books, and, until comparatively recent times
when enlightened men were inspired to climb upon them
for pleasure and exercise, it was fashionable to regard
them as objects of awe and terror, and their summits
were rarely visited. Not so High Street, which has been
known and trodden, down through the ages, by a
miscellany of travellers on an odd variety of missions:
by marching soldiers, marauding brigands, carousing
shepherds, officials of the Governments, and now by
modern hikers.'
A. Wainwright

*An aerial view of Haweswater Reservoir showing the wooded promontory
known as 'The Rigg'*

This walk begins in a remote spot in the far eastern area of the lakes, in the Haweswater Valley. As the name of this fell suggests this is quite literally a 'high street', an ancient route well trodden for at least 2,000 years. So, my goal was not simply to reach its summit, but to also discover how legions of Roman soldiers who trudged across this glorious fell, fired the imagination of the young Alfred Wainwright.

The name High Street intrigued Wainwright so much so that he climbed it during his first visit to the Lakes in 1930 when he was just twenty-three. High Street gets its name from the Roman road which once ran across the fell tops and through the valleys between two forts at Ambleside and near Penrith. Beginning the walk on the quiet shores of Haweswater Reservoir it is easy to see how Wainwright would have been captivated by the isolated beauty and tranquility of this small valley. It's very quiet here and the immediacy of the fells is so dramatic. But, behind all of this grand scenery hides a very intriguing story. Haweswater itself may look like an unspoilt stretch of Lakeland Valley, but the view here is almost entirely manmade.

Back along the Mardale Road, sits an enormous dam. It was built in 1935 and turned the valley's natural lake into a huge reservoir that could supply drinking water to Manchester. But beneath the surface lie the flooded remains of Mardale Green and Measand.

You might expect there to have been some resistance to this project from the locals and the villagers. But, after parliament passed an Act giving the Manchester Corporation permission to flood the Mardale Valley the controversial construction of the Haweswater Dam began in 1929. It was described as a 'monstrous plug' at the time but it didn't stir the level of protest you might expect of such an invasive project. This was, after all, just after World War I and there was very little for the men to come back to and this would

An aerial view of Haweswater leading to its dam. Hundreds and thousands of gallons of water are now pumped out to service homes in the northwest
Right: An aerial view of the ridge walk which leads upwards from 'The Rigg'

provide 200 jobs. I suspect that for a lot of people it perhaps seemed a positive step as it would generate much needed work.

The Mardale Valley was chosen because the original Haweswater was the highest lake in England, about 700 feet above sea level, which was really important in the logistics of getting water the eighty odd miles down to Manchester.

But before these dramatic changes swept in this was simple farming country. It's hard to imagine today that about half way between the wooded headland, known as 'The Rigg', and the other side was the site of the Dun Bull Pub. This promonontory would also have looked very different. In the 30s, by the time Wainwright would have seen it, it was basically down to about forty inhabitants, a Vicarage and apparently a beautiful little Church, one of the smallest in the Lake District. In August 1935 the last service was held. Tickets were issued for a seventy-five strong congregation,

but in fact eighty-one squeezed in the door and all the others were outside. It is said that as they sang the hymn, 'Lift up thine eyes to the hills' the tears that were shed were the first tears of the reservoir.

The buildings here were then by and large demolished; the Territorial Army apparently even came in to practice detonation procedures on them. Only the Church was spared and that was taken down stone by stone and quite a lot of the materials were used to build the Dwarf Tower for the reservoir, which is the tower-like structure you see half way down.

Rather more gruesomely the hundred bodies buried in the Churchyard were all exhumed and taken to Shap, where a special little area in the cemetery was made over to former residents of the Mardale Valley.

In times of drought I've been told you can still see walls, roads and little piles of stones. But the upside of this stark and sad story is that today the reservoir at least lives up to its purpose. Hundreds of thousands of gallons are now pumped south every day. At its maximum capacity this reservoir can hold 18.6 billion gallons of water, roughly enough to give everyone on the planet three baths!

Wainwright was however, particularly clear about his preferred route from Mardale despite this rather ghostly start, describing it is as the 'the connoisseur's route up High Street.' He was emphatic in his preferred choice, stating: 'The ascent is a classic, leading directly along the crest of a long, straight ridge that permits of no variation from the valley to the summit. The views are excellent throughout.'

The first port of call is the promontory at the edge of Haweswater known as 'The Rigg'. It's hard to believe that not so long ago this once looked out onto fields and cottages.

The route may be fairly straightforward but from 'The Rigg' the path is not, it's all twists and turns and there are loads of rocks, which make it really hard going and may slow you down quite a lot. Once you reach around 1,600 feet (488 metres) the view really opens out on both sides. The dam is off to the northeast and if you look down you should just be able to make out the small manmade islet of Wood Howe. It was built to mimic similar scenery at the natural lakes of Windermere and Derwentwater to ensure that this reservoir blended in with the overall Lakeland landscape.

As the path steepens and you reach the top of the crag you will be rewarded with clear views into the valleys on both sides of the ridge and the first view of the summit (although from here I should warn you it still looks tiny – there's still a way to go).

From this ridge you will also be able see the other valley, Riggindale, to the north. As you progress along the ridge, each high point has its own name, with Swine, Heron and Eagle Crag all to be ticked off.

Wainwright wrote about being in this same spot: 'I was

Blea Water
Crag

standing here a few years ago, looking down into Riggindale, when a huge bird took off from the crags below and with two lazy flaps of its wings soared effortlessly across the valley and alighted on the topmost rocks of Kidsty Pike opposite. There was no doubting its identity. It was a Golden Eagle.'

The sight of eagles was once commonplace across Lakeland. Haweswater is the last place in England where the Golden Eagle nested and sadly, the valley's ageing solo male, has been without a mate since 2004.

Although I wasn't lucky enough to spot this lone Eagle, there is one unusual Lakeland view here that you are guaranteed. Looking out from the ridge, there are two tarns in one view. Small Water nestled below Harter Fell, and the larger Blea Water. Not only is this one of the most impressive tarns in the Lake District, it is also the deepest, plunging to 207 feet (63 metres). It is also the third deepest body of water in the Lakes, only Wastwater (74 metres) and Lake Windermere (67 metres) are deeper.

The top of High Street may be in sight, but the path is still interrupted by the seemingly endless rocky spine of

An aerial view of High Street's 'Racecourse Hill' the section between the summit and the Straits of Riggindale

Rough Crag. Every time you get over one of its mini summits there seems to be another one. The summit of Rough Crag will soon be reached but it's really just a knobble on this huge undulating ridge and the cairn is a rather pitiful

pile of rocks. As you pass over each of the crags there is a brief moment of descent providing a little respite. But you will keep spying the summit of High Street looming ominously above.

The last drag is rather a cruel one, just as you think you're nearly there, there's one more shift upwards. But once you reach Long Stile it means the next spot is definitely, definitely the summit.

Long Stile buttresses the enormous grassy plateau of High Street and forms the final chapter of this walk up the ridge. The long flat top of the fell is where the Roman road reaches its highest point as it passes from north to south. On a clear day the edge of the summit plateau gives amazing views back along the ridge to Haweswater.

Julia slowly ascends Rough Crag and Long Stile

At this point you are around 2,461 feet (750 metres) above sea level, which means this is the highest piece of Roman road in Britain. It was constructed to link the Roman fort at Broom, in the north, near Penrith, with the Roman forts of Ambleside and Keswick, in the south. It was probably built around the end of the first century. The Romans apparently used local materials that were easily at hand, which makes an awful lot of sense when you're working at this height. But don't expect to find a cobbled surface or a long straight track. This road looks slightly more organic. To build it, the Romans levelled out the surface by removing a layer of peat. They then dumped on individual layers of gravel, peat, brushwood and finally an overall covering of larger stones. Apparently it is very similar to the technique of pitching that the National Park and the National Trust use today when they are repairing upland footpaths.

But it wasn't just the Romans who came here, something else that Wainwright picks up on. High Street was also the site of annual fairs and shepherd gatherings. The shepherds needed to get together at certain times of the year, largely to

THE SUMMIT

return sheep that had strolled over one valley to the next. So they would all get together on the same day and returned stock that had strayed. But the most important aspect of this was the social dimension and it would seem there was a great deal of merriment with lots of eating, drinking and feasting. The most memorable aspect of this was the athletics and games. The thing that made the games on High Street quite so unique was that they featured a horse race. When you stand up there you can certainly begin to conjure up an amazing image of people galloping down the straits between High Street and Riggindale, which is a steep slope (quite a test of nerve). The name 'Racecourse Hill' is still preserved today.

Being right on the eastern edge of the Lakes, this is a fantastic place to see all the giants of Lakeland along the horizon in a long and ordered line. There's Skiddaw, then Helvellyn, the upside down basin that's Great Gable and even Scafell Pike.

As Wainwright frequently remarks, there is something unspoiled and special about this now remote frontier area of the national park. Despite its long and crowded history, the High Street range can still be walked from dawn to dusk without meeting another soul.

Of all the large plateau summits I've visited, High Street is undoubtedly one of the most remarkable. Not only is it simply enormous, a 'whaleback' as Wainwright described it, but it's also a place of a thousand stories, lost secrets, history. No wonder that when Wainwright first visited here he became so fired up by it. It really is an evocative fell both grand and wild and one that will stir the imagination.

Julia's tips for a tipple:

The Kirkstone Pass Inn, (Ambleside/Patterdale Road) is a fine old pub for walkers and families which serves food.

PILLAR

PILLAR

Julia's Overview

This was the final Wainwright summit that I tackled for the television series and whilst it's not the highest it certainly felt like a fitting end. This route, more than any other, is a truly remote mountain adventure. Getting to the start alone requires some dedication, never mind the physical effort which this 'overlord of the western scene' demands. Ennerdale where we began our day is remote. Properly remote. No road access, no people, no buildings – except the Black Sail Youth Hostel, an old shepherds' shelter that has been there for hundreds of years. I've filmed there several times over the years and it is picture postcard stuff. 'If Carlsberg built youth hostels' they'd all look like this...

This route took us into the deep heart of AW's cherished Lakeland landscape and then we got out of there as fast as possible! A lighting storm began to threaten in the distance and then big black clouds started zooming towards us. I've never seen David Powell-Thompson (our mountain guide) move so quickly off a mountain. Jan the cameraman pointed out to Clare our sound lady that she was the tallest thing on the mountain – standing there like a pylon with her boom pole in the air – 'You do realise that if anyone gets struck by lightening it'll be you?' We made our swift exit down the fellrunners path and I don't think I stopped for breath.

This remote outpost is as far flung from the pretty tea parlours and gift shops of the tourist hubs as you can hope to be. So perhaps it was on this walk, more than any other, that the true scale of AW's endeavour became clear.

Julia above the Ennerdale Valley
Pages 174-175: Pillar photographed from Wasdale Head

This uncluttered spot shows off so supremely a seemingly never-ending vista of fells, most of which AW roamed and dedicated the best part of his life to. Walking each of these paths and reaching the many summits is achievement alone, but to leave a legacy of seven books of his observations and annotations is a gift indeed, a unique and almost unfathomable legacy to be shared, cherished and admired by generations of walkers to come. Just don't get struck by lightning.

PILLAR

ASCENT FROM ENNERDALE
(BLACK SAIL YOUTH HOSTEL)
2000 feet of ascent : 2¾ miles
(2100 feet, 3 miles
by High Level Route)

PILLAR

2700
2600
2500
2400

Great
Doup

Pillar Rock

stretcher box

Hind
Cove

grass

2300

Green
Cove

Robinson's
Cairn

High Level Route

← detail →

1
2
3
4
5

Looking
Stead

WASDALE HEAD
direct route

1900

tarn

WASDALE
HEAD

1800

Black Sail
Pass

1700

1600

Main ridge:
1 : zigzag path
2 : direct path
High Level route:
3 : original start
4 : new variation
Main ridge:
5 : from Black Sail

Ash
Crag

1500
1400
1300
1200

River Liza

Sail Beck

1100

Black
Sail
Y.H.

1000

moraines

THE WALK
Pillar – from Ennerdale (Black Sail Youth Hostel)

SUMMIT HEIGHT: *2,927 feet/892 metres*
(2,100 feet/640 metres of ascent)
DISTANCE: *3 miles/4.8 kilometres*
OS MAP: *OL4*
Pictorial Guide Book Seven – The Western Fells

'Soujourners at the hostel are fortunate in having Pillar on their doorstep, and can enjoy one of the best days of their young lives by climbing it.'
A. Wainwright

OVERVIEW

Leaving Black Sail Youth Hostel you head further up the valley to cross the River Liza. The bridge then takes you onto the path up to Black Sail Pass, a broad grassy slope and the quickest route over the hills to the Wasdale Valley. But as you reach the top of the Pass you turn northwest and step onto the main ridge that leads all the way to the summit. The path passes close to the grassy dome of Looking Stead, Wainwright's recommended viewpoint for the whole of Ennerdale. This is close to where I left the ridge and set off on the High Level Route, which cuts across Pillar's dramatic north face. Along here the cliffs continue to grow in size, until a long diagonal ledge known as the Shamrock Traverse gives walkers the chance to come face to face with Pillar Rock, Wainwright's most 'handsome crag'. But this rock is not the top, there's a challenging end before you've conquered the north face with another 400 feet (122 metres) of steep scrambling to go. Only then do you emerge on top and you will be able to walk across Pillar's rounded peak.

The Walk

'Pillar, in fact, far from being a spire of slender
proportions, is a rugged mass broadly based on
half the length of Ennerdale, a series of craggy
buttresses supporting the ridge high above this
wild north face; and the summit itself, far from
being pointed is wide and flat.'
A. Wainwright

An aerial view of Ennerdale Water

Opting to begin this walk at the very tip of the Ennerdale Valley takes you to one of the remotest spots in the Lake District. From Black Sail Youth Hostel it's 9 miles (14.4 kilometres) to the nearest village, and at least 5 miles (8 kilometres) to a proper tarmac road. Dominating the side of the Ennerdale Valley is Pillar, the highest peak in the western fells. Just short of 3,000 feet (914 metres), Pillar is right up there amongst England's highest summits. But it's in terms of drama that Alfred Wainwright thought this mountain really excelled. His description does justice to its bold shapeliness: 'The north face of the fell has a formidable aspect. Crags and shadowed hollows, scree and tumbled boulders, form a wild, chaotic scene, a setting worthy of a fine mountain.'

At the heart of the north face stands Pillar Rock, a 500-foot (152-metre) tower, the defining feature of the mountain. Wainwright mapped a High Level Route that could take determined walkers right through this dramatic scenery. But this is a real mountain expedition and anyone wanting to tackle it with plenty of daylight on their side may want an early start.

Thanks to the Black Sail Youth Hostel, this is certainly made possible. This squat little stone building is a sort of outpost of civilization in this valley, a definite favourite of Wainwright's and just about anybody hoping to get the best out of Ennerdale will make a beeline for it.

Black Sail is the only building in the upper reaches of Ennerdale. It may not be five star accommodation, but that will probably be of little concern to you, given that the location is unsurpassed. Walkers who've already trekked for miles to get here, can sit and assess their route up Pillar, with little more than the grazing sheep to disturb them. When you come here you know you're only ever going to share the valley with a handful of people.

The valley has such atmosphere at anytime of the day or year, whatever the weather, even when the wind is whistling around and the slates on the roof are rattling. I don't think you could ever get bored of the view either. Being at Black Sail means you are already 900 feet (274 metres) above sea level, right amongst the high ground at the end of the valley (making it one of the shortest distances I'd ever had to cover to reach one of country's highest peaks).

Once you leave the youth hostel, the approach to Black Sail Pass takes you towards the dome shaped summit of Pillar's largest neighbour, Great Gable. Kirk Fell is to the right, Green Gable to the left. These three shapely summits form a sort of natural blockade that have helped preserve the total isolation of this spot.

From here, you can also stand and look over thousands of conifers that fill the valley floor all the way to Ennerdale Water. By the time Wainwright arrived here, the trees had already been planted to replenish wood reserves after World War I.

But he clearly wasn't a fan: 'Afforestation in Ennerdale has cloaked the lower slopes in a dark and funereal shroud of foreign trees, an intrusion that nobody who knew Ennerdale of old can ever forgive...'

The long steady climb up Black Sail Pass is hot work and you will no doubt experience that familiar problem of what to wear. I seemed to be forever stop starting, taking one layer off and then adding another. As you steadily get higher, the

Black Sail Youth Hostel a remote outpost in the Ennerdale Valley

wind can certainly bite every time you pause for breath and as you look back over your shoulder Black Sail base camp gets further and further away.

The top end of this pass is where the air gets channelled between Pillar and Kirk Fell, a well-trodden route once taken by shepherds and miners alike heading towards Wasdale and the Cumbrian coastline. Wainwright advises to look for a gate, which marks the top of the pass but suggests: 'Only a fanatical purist would think of using it'. It's been over forty years since this book was originally written, and when I visited, the gate still hadn't been fixed.

As the route veers north it takes you onto a broad ridge and the approach slopes of Pillar. This is where Wainwright's eye for detail and artistry come to the fore. If you look at page ten of his Pillar description and the way he's angled the drawing and its scale he managed to fit a very intense, complex, curvy route all onto one pocket-sized page.

Julia enjoys the view from Looking Stead

It's at this stage of the route that things start to get pretty interesting.

From the small, unnamed tarn, the broad grassy ridge stretches out for another half a mile (0.8 kilometres). You can stride out with the view down into Wasdale opening up on your left. But it's to the other side of the ridge that AW suggests a brief detour. Looking Stead is a small pinnacle jutting out, 1,000 feet (305 metres) below the main summit. It's also an ideal vantage point to assess the view down into Ennerdale, one of Lakeland's more controversial valleys.

From up here you can really see the work that's being done in Ennerdale at the moment. Huge swathes of conifers have clearly been taken out. Acres of evergreen forest give Ennerdale a rather unfamiliar look. More Canadian Rockies than English Lakes and a scene which Wainwright did not find altogether agreeable. He wrote: 'It is an offence to the eyes to see Pillar's once-colourful fellside now hobbled in such a dowdy and ill-suited skirt...Yet such is the majesty and

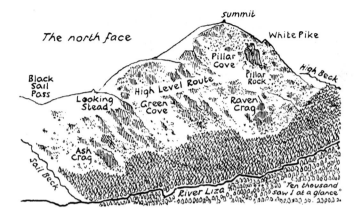

power of this fine mountain that it can shrug off the insults and indignities, and its summit soars no less proudly above.' But you imagine that AW would have been quite pleased with the current 'Wild Ennerdale' project, a scheme, which is steadily removing conifers and introducing areas of mixed woodland. In years to come the valley should have a more natural beauty to accompany one of Wainwright's favourite mountains.

You will also soon get your first view of the drama of the High Level Route cutting across the rocks and cliffs of the north face of Pillar. But before this diversion, the grassy eastern slopes of Pillar are a simple fellwalking pleasure (although do keep your eyes peeled for a rather fine view at about 2,000 feet (607 metres). You can look down the opposite valley, all the way to the head of Wastwater, the deepest lake in England).

But the route is about to change. Walkers after a real adventure should now look for the easily missed diversion. As the grand peak of Scafell appears in the background, there's a small cairn, which indicates the turning point for the High Level Route.

Julia reaches the top of Shamrock Traverse and discovers Pillar Rock, 'the most handsome crag in the Lakes'

Wainwright thought this was the start of one the best miles in Lakeland, a route of engrossing interest. To kick things off, whilst the main path continues up, the High Level Route takes you down...steeply down.

Stepping onto the north face of Pillar is like making a leap to an entirely new mountain. This really can't be described as a 'walk' any longer. This is a true and testing fell climb. Your gaze may well be tempted up to the ever-heightening peaks above, but be warned, you can't absently mindedly stroll along the High Level Route. Every ten metres or so there's something new to negotiate, scree, boulders and occasional outbreaks of very wet rocks.

The High Level Route twists and turns its way around the many spurs and buttresses that support the mountain. Unlike the ridge path far above, there's rarely a chance for an unobstructed view. But there is one large manmade feature to look out for.

East Face of High Man

as seen from the Shamrock Traverse.

Robinson's Cairn is Wainwright's final significant landmark before you get to Pillar Rock. John Wilson Robinson was a local man and a pioneer of rock-climbing who established many of the now famous routes up Pillar Rock. When he died a century ago, his friends came here to build a cairn in his honour.

It's a good goal to aim for because you are rewarded with a view towards Pillar Rock. Robinson's Cairn is the first place where you begin to see how a mere walker can hope to negotiate Pillar Rock. From here you can just make out the rest of the path and Shamrock Traverse, the steep and narrow ledge that leads you almost level with the topmost pinnacle of Pillar Rock.

It is in fact from this pinnacle that the whole mountain derives its name. Wainwright explains: 'The Rock, despite a remote and lonely situation had a well-established local notoriety and fame long before tourists called wider attention to it and an object of such unique appearance simply had to be given a descriptive name, although at the time, one was not yet needed to identify the mountain of which it formed part. The Pillar was an inspiration of shepherds. Men of letters could not have chosen better.' And so it was that the Lake District's most notorious rock formation became the name for an entire mountain. From here onwards it begins to dominate your horizon, a full 500 feet (152 metres) from base to summit.

Gradually the Rock seems to block out the sunlight as you climb a section of scree to get onto Shamrock Traverse. Excluding the summits, Wainwright rated this spot as one of his favourite places in the whole of Lakeland and it's certainly an experience. Loose stones, a big drop and a narrow ledge add a certain amount of adrenalin-fuelled excitement to this section of the route.

The vast majority of other ascents up Pillar never come anywhere near this level of high drama. It's an ingenious route, allowing fellwalkers a rare chance to scale vertical cliff faces and as Wainwright points out 'the rock scenery is magnificent.' The name Shamrock however has nothing to do with Irish clover leaves. It is, quite literally a 'sham' rock. From a distance it appears to be part of the same crag as Pillar Rock, but as you reach its top, you realise the two are separated by a mighty chasm. Once you've twinkle toed your way across the traverse one of the most handsome crags in Lakeland is now staring you in the face. But as Wainwright makes unusually clear, this is as close as one gets without ropes and a harness.

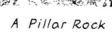

A Pillar Rock

He emphatically states: 'Pillar Rock is positively out of bounds. Don't even try to get a foothold on it. The climbing guides mention easy routes but these are not easy for a walker who is not a climber, and lead into dangerous situations.'

Rock climbers, or 'crag rats' as they're known in these parts, have been drawn to Pillar throughout the ages. The main jagged peak at the centre was first conquered in 1826. This route takes you past the peak of Pillar Rock traversing the top of Walker's Gully. But rather like the Rock, this is actually no place for walkers, quite the opposite in fact. This ever-steepening crack is where a man named Walker once tried to descend the mountain, a decision that tragically cost him his life.

Above the rock the ascent can suddenly feel rather more exposed. There's a direct climb of 400 feet (122 metres) left, offering some pretty intense scrambling. But this is the final hurdle on your approach the summit. After all that climbing and all those rocks you eventually pop out on top to find a surprisingly flat summit.

But with the expanse of this broad peak there are also sweeping and majestic views. Finally you can look down onto Ennerdale Water and on a very clear day if you look round to the north you might even spy Scotland as well as the entire Cumbrian coastline. From here the giant tops of Scafell and Scafell Pike can also be spotted and many more of the vast number of peaks charted in detail by AW.

Julia's tips for a tipple:

Options include Wasdale Head Inn (Wasdale), The Shepherd's Arms, and The Fox & Hounds (Ennerdale Bridge).

Julia Bradbury Titles Available on DVD and Blu-ray

Wainwright Walks
Series One and Two
DVD £19.99
AV9917

Wainwright Walks
Coast to Coast
DVD £11.99
AV9676

Wainwright Walks
Complete Collection
DVD £34.99
AV9590

Railway Walks with
Julia Bradbury
DVD £11.99
AV9677
Blu-ray £14.99
AB2001

Canal Walks with
Julia Bradbury
DVD £14.99
AV9827
Blu-ray £14.99
AB2003

German Wanderlust
with Julia Bradbury
DVD £12.99
AV9801

South Africa Walks
with Julia Bradbury
DVD £11.99
AV9762

Secret Britain with
Julia Bradbury
and Matt Baker
DVD £12.99
AV3036

The Great British
Countryside with
Julia Bradbury
and Hugh Dennis
DVD £14.99
AV3035

Order now from www.acornmediauk.com or telephone
the UK customer orderline on 0333 123 2312.